Reaching Through the Veil to Heal

About the Author

Linda Drake (Austin, Texas) is an author, teacher, and life path healer who has dedicated her life to working with Spirit. She travels worldwide helping people heal the physical and emotional challenges in their lives, including relationship and childhood issues. Linda does her healing work through her books, seminars, workshops, and private sessions. She is a Reiki Master and channels Spirit energy to bring balance and healing to the entire body. If you would like to contact her, you can write to her through her website, www.lindadrakebooks.com. You can also visit her website for the latest news and locations of special in-person appearances. If you are interested in scheduling a workshop in your area, please contact her.

Death, Grief & Communicating

REACHING THROUGH THE VEIL TO HEAL

with Loved Ones in Spirit

Linda Drake

Llewellyn Publications
Woodbury, Minnesota

First Edition
Second Printing, 2007

Cover art © 2006 by Jui Ishida
Cover design by Gavin Dayton Duffy
Llewellyn is a registered trademark of Llewellyn Worldwide, Ltd.

Library of Congress Cataloging-in-Publication Data (Pending)
ISBN 13: 978-0-7387-0932-1
ISBN 10: 0-7387-0932-8

Llewellyn Publications
A Division of Llewellyn Worldwide, Ltd.
2143 Wooddale Drive, Dept. 0-7387-0932-8
Woodbury, Minnesota 55125-2989, U.S.A.
www.llewellyn.com

Printed in the United States of America

Dedication and Acknowledgments

To Pat Drake, my husband, best friend, and soul mate: God knew it would take a very special person to love and support me in all that God and I had chosen for my life path. It had to be a "special order," but God created that very person just for me. Thank you for loving me just the way I am and for doing such a great job of it.

To my daughters, Tammye, Laurie, Heather, and Emily: Being a mom and stepmom gave me a wealth of knowledge and compassion for the parents that would eventually be coming to me for guidance. Motherhood has been a wonderful experience, but being Grandma is a lot easier. Thank you for your love and support. Even though you may not understand my unusual perspective on life, you continue to laugh with me, always helping me enjoy the adventures of my life.

As human beings, we are each given spiritual gifts. One of the gifts that God gave to me is the ability to communicate with and channel groups of angels and masters, as well as Spirit. One of those groups is Abraham. Abraham is a collective consciousness of highly evolved beings. They share their wisdom to guide us along the paths we have chosen for our lives. That wisdom was channeled through me into the writing of this book, along with the wisdom of Spirit.

I thank Spirit and Abraham for allowing me to be a part of the writing of this book and the many books to come. It is such an honor and pleasure to share their knowledge and the healing energy that this book holds.

I thank Spirit for having faith in me, and I pray that I will be a worthy servant in carrying Spirit's gift of healing to each of you through this book.

I thank the wonderful individuals who helped edit this book, making it all come together and flow. I especially thank Mary Ellen Keith and Hilda McKethan for their hard work and grammatical knowledge.

I thank all of my clients: Spirit allowed me to be a part of your healing experience, and you trusted me to touch your souls in a very unusual way. I experienced tremendous spiritual growth and learned so much as I assisted Spirit in helping you all attain the healing your hearts desired. You have definitely blessed my life and made my work interesting.

I especially thank those of you who have shared your healing experiences through this book. Spirit tells me that the thoughts, emotions, and healing that you shared in your stories will contribute greatly to the healing energy of this book. This knowledge will enable others to gain a better understanding of the challenges of their lives and find their own healing experience.

I dedicate this book to everyone who has experienced the anguish of losing a loved one. May your heart be touched, comforted, and healed through the messages we bring to you in this book.

May God bless and heal you.

Contents

Introduction

I am an intuitive life path healer, having worked with Spirit as a healer for many years. Spirit came into my life quite suddenly after I was miraculously healed of two life-debilitating diseases, an experience that convinced me to walk the healing path with Spirit. During a "near death experience," I was shown the purpose of my life.

I have become a true channel for Spirit, using my intuitive gifts of clairvoyance and clairaudience. In doing my work, I channel Spirit healing energy along with Reiki energy, devoting my life to helping others heal and connecting my clients with their angels, guides, and Spirit, who give their guidance and healing. I work closely with the angelic realm, allowing me to connect with loved ones and friends who have passed over. This in itself brings great healing to those on both sides. I have traveled the world sharing my healing gifts and messages; in doing Spirit's work, I have touched thousands of lives. In my lectures I channel a collective consciousness that call themselves Abraham. My books are channeled from Abraham and Spirit, bringing healing words of wisdom that will touch your heart and give you the tools to change your life, as well as give you confirmation of your own spiritual path.

When Spirit first told me I would be writing a book, I laughed and protested that I had no writing skills and I certainly had no amazing knowledge to share. They told me not to fear, because I would not be writing the book by myself. They said Abraham would be channeling it to me. That gave me great comfort, as I had been working with Abraham for many years. Spirit fulfilled their promise, and the Abraham consciousness group showed up to write each morning. That is how this book was created.

In this book, we will explore the disappointments, losses, and abandonment that we experience throughout our lives that prepare us for our greatest losses and that teach us to allow others to help us through these difficult life challenges. The goal of this book is to help you look at the grief that comes with the loss of a loved one through death or illness and the loss of relationships or jobs, all of which are part of life but can impact our lives in devastating ways. We hope to give you a better understanding of grief—what it is, how it affects your life, and how you can move forward through the healing process.

The death of a loved one is the greatest of losses, plunging a person into the depths of shock, numbness, and disbelief as they begin their long journey through grief. Many other losses can create some of these same emotions, as we must work our way through similar stages of grief.

Few of us walk through life without having to experience grief at some point. Grief is a part of life, but seldom do we understand the complexities of the experience. What is grief? How do we handle all of the intense emotions that go along with it? Rarely are we prepared for the emotions that are created by death and grief, as we are thrust into the depths of emotion, beyond the boundaries of our everyday experiences. The loss of a loved one may evoke emotions you may have never felt before, or at least not to that extent. It can be very frightening and unnerving as we move through these unfamiliar emotions in a way that we feel we have no control over.

We each experience grief in our own way, but the common thread involves pain—a pain that can affect our lives physically, emotionally, and spiritually. Grief is a process we go through, lasting no set time and having no rules. It is inevitable that we will change, as many of us feel there is an empty place within us following our loss. We question how we can function without the energy of this person in our lives. You may struggle with how to say goodbye, how to let go, how to move on without the physical presence of this person in your life. It is unrealistic to believe that life will stay the same without this person. No matter what position your loved one played in your life, there will be an empty place that they once filled for you.

We hope to give you a different perspective, helping you understand that your loved one has not left you, at least not on the spiritual level. Their energy can still be with you, just in a different form. They are now part of your support system. They will walk with you through your many stages of grief, holding your hand and crying with you, as they whisper words of love and encouragement to your heart. They will be there when you are ready to move forward, cheering you on and helping you through your time of healing, as you become stronger and grow to embrace the changes in your life.

In my personal healing work with clients, I use a very nurturing, down-to-earth approach that I share in this book, guiding the reader through the healing experiences of my clients. To enlighten my readers and clients about the spiritual world, I channel Spirit's words of guidance as they lead each of us down our spiritual paths.

Linda and Spirit's Introduction to Death, Grief, and Healing with the Other Side

Through reading this book, you will better understand life, death, grief, and the healing process. The purpose is not to dredge up painful buried emotions, but rather to help you acknowledge, heal, and release those with whom *you* have not completed your healing process. Those in spirit form prefer being referred to as "in spirit" as opposed to "dead," because we as a society hold so many misconceptions about death. Don't get me wrong—they don't oppose being dead. They just don't like being called "dead" because of our fear of death, and they do not want us to fear them or the process. They desire that we have a better understanding about what death is and how it works.

In this book, when I am speaking of the energy of the God consciousness, I refer to it as Spirit with a capital *S*. But when I am referring to the human soul, I refer to that spirit with a small *s*.

When I am talking about Spirit, I am referring to a combination of energies, made up of the God consciousness, the Masters, and those of the angelic realm. I am told that the Masters speak the words of God, helping us better understand God's desires for us. The angels are the fingers of God, doing his work within our lives. They all work together to give us a better understanding of who we are and the purpose of our existence. This combination of Spirit is part of our soul's support system, along with our own angels and spirit guides. God created humanity, giving us the ability to co-create the future of our lives. God also gave us very powerful support systems to assist us in whatever we choose to experience.

chapter one

Our Life Purpose

We all come into this lifetime with a life plan. It has a beginning and an ending. There are those who believe that your date of death is set at the time you enter, but Spirit explains this to me in a slightly different way.

I am told that we have an approximate life span, with several exit points built into it. The choices we make during our lives determine the exact length of our time here. We come into this lifetime with a long list of things that we want to accomplish. Our soul, or higher self, is very motivated for growth and advancement of karmic healing in this lifetime. You created karma with those in your soul group, as well as people from other soul groups, throughout many lifetimes. In each additional lifetime, you are given the opportunity to heal what you created in past lifetimes.

Karma is energy that you have the choice of creating through your actions. You can create either negative or positive energy, but whichever energy you create, it will be returned to you in that same form. You will be given opportunities to heal your karma or help someone else heal the karma that they created.

Our life plan also includes a long list of people, especially those of our soul group, with whom we have previously agreed to interact in this lifetime. God gave us (humanity) free will to create our lives and to make our own choices, but we must learn that each choice will carry consequences. It is best if we can learn this principle of cause and effect early in our lives. To illustrate this principle, Spirit shows me the vision of a stone being dropped into a pool of water, and how its ripple effect changes the energy of the entire body of water. This is how the choices we make affect us and all of those around us. No matter how large or small the stone, the energy or choices it creates will affect others; this is how karma works.

I have been with people who appeared to be on death's doorstep, but who nonetheless continued to live. When I questioned Spirit about this miraculous recovery, they explained to me that it was not that person's time to leave. The purpose of the illness was to bring an issue to their attention, giving them and those around them the opportunity to learn something from the experience and the emotions the experience created. Sometimes, when a person is close to death and it may be their time to leave, they are given an extension of time in which to accomplish something that has been left undone. It is not unusual to see those who are near death given extra days as an opportunity to say goodbye or to heal some issue with family members. I am told that their soul actually has this choice, showing us that even in death God gives us choices.

Our higher self/soul knows the timing of our impending death, and our soul begins to prepare us in subtle ways. Our consciousness is seldom aware of the decisions that we make leading up to the destiny of our death. When looking back at choices made or the actions people have taken even prior to an unexpected death, we will often see a level of preparation that even the dying person was unaware of.

A loved one may seem to have died in an accidental way, but the timing of the death was not an accident. The experience of their death was only the vehicle through which they left. It was part of their life plan. What others experience through their loved one's life and death is part of their own life purpose.

For the completion of our life purpose, we are given assistance by Spirit, our angels, guides, and loved ones in spirit. This is a very powerful group that God has given us. We need to value and draw upon their wisdom and guidance.

There is a purpose for *every* challenge that we endure in our life, right up to our death. Sometimes, as the soul understands that it is time to leave, the person may choose to go suddenly, because they do not wish to endure the trauma and suffering of a prolonged death, or they do not want their family to have to endure it. The soul understands death, and there is no fear, because the soul sees death as the completion of a plan.

For many years I have been working with people, helping them heal all types of issues. My work is channeled from Spirit, so it is not my knowledge, but the power of Spirit, that will assist you in your healing. We do not do the healing for you; rather, we assist you in releasing the mental, emotional, or physical blockages that are preventing you from healing yourself. God created the human body as an energy-being, able to heal itself. He provided this healing ability through the function of the chakra system. Chakras are the power points in your body that generate a life force energy that provides the human body with the necessary energy of life. This energy works to maintain your bodily functions, to sustain life, and to heal the body itself. The chakra system can become energetically blocked or weakened by stress, trauma, illness, or negative emotions. The energy of the emotional memories (positive and negative) of our child-hood is held in these chakras. An accumulation of negative energy creates a blockage, preventing the body from being able to heal a disease or to release pain from an injury. This negative energy can also be held in the cellular structure of the body as well as in the chakra system. These nega-tive energies must be released to enable us to heal. Grief is a trauma that can weaken or block the energy of the chakra system.

Spirit uses many different healing methods. We use Reiki and Spirit energy in combination with other healing tools to help our clients. Com-municating with the other side is also a very powerful healing tool. I will be sharing with you stories that my clients have written about their healing experiences. I have changed the names to protect their privacy. I understand that some stories may challenge your belief system, but they are all true.

For some of you, death is a very sensitive subject at this time, since you may have recently suffered through the trauma of losing someone close to you. Certainly, the experience of this loss makes you very aware of the many different emotions we experience as we move through the grieving process. If this is the case for you, I encourage you to read the book slowly, processing the information as you go along.

When I invited my clients to share their experiences with grief and their healing stories through my book, I had no idea what beautiful sto-ries would come forth. Each time I sit down with someone and open the doorway to the other side, I always ask in prayer that healing will occur for all parties involved in whatever way they need it. I trust this to be Spir-it's gift to us, as I have witnessed tremendous healing come to souls on both sides when given the opportunity to interact after death. Through their stories, my clients have generously agreed to share their healing ex-periences with you. I guarantee that you will laugh, that you will cry, and that they will touch your heart.

We will begin with Sherri's story. I first met Sherri at a psychic fair where I was doing intuitive readings. The psychic fairs I attend are very spiritual events where like-minded people gather to share their intuitive, God-given gifts. Quite often, during the readings in which I give my clients messages from their angels and spirit guides, a loved one in spirit will come from the other side to give a message. This is what happened for Sherri. Her deceased mother came forward and gave words of love and encouragement. A few days later I received a call from Sherri saying she wanted to give her father a session with me for his birthday. I was delighted to be a part of the healing that came through that session. Here is her story. In this particular story I have left the names and places as Sherri wrote them.

Reunion on Rainbow Bridge: My Parents' Journey Beyond Death

I look at my father, Jim Swanson, as he stares out the window, and I see the undeniable grief that fills his eyes. Where once there was an irrepressible twinkle, now only a sad stare remains. He grieves for my mother, Shirley, who finally succumbed to the torment of kidney disease five years ago. I offer him a penny for his thoughts, and he tells me he is thinking about the last real conversation they had before the respirator tube took away his sweetheart's voice.

It was, he said, close to the end, when they could no longer ignore the knock at death's door. In a very private time and place—the place where their deepest desires and darkest secrets reside—they began to reflect upon their forty-six years together as husband and wife. It was like a pre-Judgment Day, especially for my mother, who had been raised as a God-fearing Southern Baptist. In particular, she wondered, would their mistakes be forgiven? Had they been good parents? Had their union really left the world a better place like, as newlyweds, they had dreamed?

The retrospective of their lives was personal, and only they could answer the poignant questions being posed, but everyone who knew them would not have any doubt about their final reckoning. Their mistakes had long been forgotten, they had been exemplary parents, and most beautiful of all was their love for each other. Without planning to, this was the legacy that, together, they would leave behind. Their love was abundant, and the way it manifested in their lives was as remarkable as how it all began in the year 1950.

Jim was seventeen years old then, full of youthful exuberance yet wise beyond his years. He had just joined the Air Force and was transferred from his native California to Barksdale Air Force Base in Bossier City, Louisiana. This was the start of a new life for the bright-eyed, golden-haired, baby-faced man. Jim was leaving behind an impoverished childhood that had ended with his dropping out of high school. He believed that the Air Force, despite the opinion of one rigid and bitter high school teacher, would recognize and encourage his fervent ambition and desire to succeed.

In that same year, Shirley had just turned fourteen years old—chronologically, just a child, but maturity-wise, already a young woman. She was a tomboy, tough and proud of it, although her appearance betrayed her. She looked like a woman in a Renaissance painting, with her alabaster skin; large, dark, almond-shaped eyes; and soft, curly, onyx-colored hair. She stood only four feet eleven inches tall and made true the saying "Dynamite comes in small packages." Her life had been difficult since her father's death when she was just two years old. Her mother, Anna, had worked tirelessly to manage the farm and the cotton field all by herself. Years of back-breaking work and picking cotton until her fingers bloodied the soft white bolls were not enough to keep the place solvent. They eventually had to sell their farm in rural Chestnut and move to Shreveport to look for work and a home. Despite the loss and adversity in her life, Shirley was a happy child—a Pollyanna of sorts, always seeing the silver lining behind life's dark clouds. At school, Shirley was studious and devoted, but during her free time, she loved nothing more than dancing and rollerskating.

Jim had never learned to skate and hesitated when a buddy from the base asked him to go to the rink in Shreveport. He only agreed after his friend told him that the rink was "packed with pretty girls wearing short skating skirts." Once there, Jim realized how true it was—gorgeous girls whizzed by and looked coyly at the new, handsome face in the crowd. Then, Jim saw Shirley.

He was so stunned by her beauty, especially her sparkling, laughing eyes, that he didn't even notice her petite, hour-glass figure under the white skating dress adorned with red heart appliqués. He stood motionless as she skated by, not even able to acknowledge her flirtatious wave. Jim's lack of response, however, didn't stop Shirley from introducing herself. She had watched him from a distance and was so struck by the goodness radiating from the stranger that she was determined to meet him. Never one to be shy or speechless, Shirley carried the conversation for both of them. By the end of the night, they knew they were destined to be together.

A whirlwind romance began, despite the intense, circumspect eye of Shirley's mother. Over the next two years, Jim and Shirley's infatuation evolved into a beautiful, abiding love. They were inseparable, until Jim received orders sending him to Offutt Air Force Base in Omaha, Nebraska.

Since the military never made exceptions to orders, and the mother of a seventeen-year-old would never allow her daughter to marry before high school graduation, Jim and Shirley realized they had to work cleverly to plan a future together. So, before Jim left town, he and Shirley became engaged with the intent to marry after she graduated.

They imagined a magical wedding day. Shirley would wear a flowing white dress and veil that would make her look like a medieval princess. In his best blue suit, which would perfectly match his ocean-blue eyes, Jim would be waiting for Shirley under the stained glass window at the altar of the Baptist church. They would be surrounded by family and fragrant yellow flowers (Shirley's favorite), and joy would fill the sanctuary.

As for their honeymoon, well, it would be a romantic drive to Omaha. Most couples would be disappointed about not traveling to an exotic destination, but not Jim and Shirley. Just being next to each other was enough to make them ecstatically happy.

It was a perfect plan—except that Shirley's mother forbade it. Shirley wouldn't be eighteen years old at the time of her high school graduation, and her mother fully intended to use the law to keep her daughter at home in Shreveport. She was Anna's baby, and Anna believed Shirley would be the child who would grow up and take care of her. If "some man" took her away, then she would be all alone. So, Anna refused to speak of any wedding plans and wouldn't even look at Shirley's exquisite engagement ring that had cost Jim three month's salary.

The tenacious teen lovers then hatched a different plan. If they had to wait until Shirley was eighteen to marry, then they would wait and elope after her birthday. Of course, this would be done over Anna's dead body, and they hoped it wouldn't come to that.

Their plan was in place. No one could stop them. They just had to wait. At least, that's what they thought. On an unusually warm winter day in January 1953, their well-thought-out plan and their fairy-tale dreams for the future were shattered in an instant.

The day before, Shirley had asked her mother if she could travel with her skating partner, David, to Dallas to watch a rollerskating competition. She was barely given permission. Anna had initially denied her request. There was traveling alone in a car with a boy to consider, as well as the dangerous big-city highways that had already claimed the life of Anna's only son, Howard, in a hit-and-run accident. But Anna finally gave in to Shirley's pleading eyes; it seemed that Shirley had a way of getting what she wanted. For a moment Shirley considered asking her mother if they could stay overnight to avoid a tiring drive home, but that would have drawn a gasp of shame and would have ended any plans before they began. So, after getting approval for the day trip, Shirley skipped away like a happy little girl, ignoring her mother's feeling of foreboding and believing nothing bad would ever happen to her.

It had been their first time to see a big city, and the sights and sounds exceeded their small-town expectations. It was late by the time David began driving home. About halfway to Shreveport, after suddenly feeling the exhaustion from their exhilarating day, Shirley began to doze off in the car. Then David also began to doze off.

They jolted awake at the crushing impact of the car with a metal bridge railing. Glass shattered as their heads hit the windshield, and metal twisted as the car flipped over repeatedly. Shirley was catapulted from the car before it careened over the steep embankment, and David was tossed about inside the car before it finally smashed into a dry creek bed. Miraculously, he climbed from the wreckage uninjured, except for a cut on his head and a mild case of shock. Shirley wasn't as lucky.

She was conscious enough to know that she couldn't feel anything below her waist, and the pain she felt above her waist was excruciating. Drifting in and out of consciousness, Shirley was aware that passersby were offering words of comfort. She didn't realize that they thought she was about to die. By the time the ambulance came, Shirley was completely unconscious. The medical examiner examined her, then pronounced her dead.

Shirley suddenly jarred to consciousness, as if her spirit was shouting, "It's not your time!" As a sheet was being pulled over her head, she panicked, and somehow found the strength to move her hand. From the corner of his eye, the coroner thought he saw the bloodied sheet move. Although he thought he had imagined the quick motion, he checked again for a pulse. Much to his surprise, he found one. With urgency and a prayer for a miracle, he sent the battered beauty to the hospital. The emergency room staff called Shirley's oldest and only sibling, Agnes. She broke the news to their mother, then to Jim.

Jim was beside himself with worry. He rushed to his commanding officer and pleaded for an immediate medical emergency transfer back to Louisiana. Since eligibility for a transfer was well-defined and Jim didn't qualify, the officer could only offer him a ten-day pass. He casually commented, "If Shirley was your wife, then I could send you back to Barksdale." With much gratitude, Jim accepted the pass, aware that an idea had been planted in his frantic mind.

He arrived the next day at the hospital in Shreveport and saw that Shirley had been placed in traction. She was strapped tightly to her bed, which wasn't a bed at all, but rather a metal gurney that only allowed her to see either the old, crumbling acoustic tiles on the ceiling or the meandering cracks covered by layers of wax on the floor. Shirley's head was bolted into a special brace, which prevented any movement of her head or spine. The doctors hoped the immobility would allow some healing to take place and prove the paralysis to be temporary, but that wasn't to be. Final tests confirmed the initial prognosis—Shirley was paralyzed from the hips down. She would never sit up. She would never walk. She would never have children. And, certainly, she had to give up any hope of being a "normal" woman, let alone a dutiful wife.

Before the doctors even finished delivering their grievous news, Shirley was already refusing to believe it—maybe it was a teenager's inability to accept such a horrific finality or maybe it was her innate optimism shooting right to the surface. If ever she needed to see a silver lining, it was now, and she was desperately searching. Shirley didn't know how, but she knew she would have a life that was more than being an invalid withering away in a state hospital somewhere.

What Jim knew for sure was that he didn't want to spend one moment, not even one breath, away from his beloved. Although he was only nineteen years old, he knew he wanted to love and care for Shirley for the rest of her life, not knowing exactly what that would entail. The doctors predicted she had about ten years left to live, based on the massive internal injuries she had sustained. Jim was determined to make those years as happy as possible, abundant with unconditional love. He gently approached her, placed his hands around her tiny, china doll face, and asked if she would still marry him.

Anna was not consulted this time. She stood beside the bed watching the extraordinary teens making a monumental, life-altering decision. She held her breath as she waited for Shirley's answer. Jim held his breath, too. Shirley, having tremendous faith in God and possessing renewed confidence in her ability to overcome any obstacle, answered with a resounding "Yes!" She didn't realize that Jim wanted them to be married before his ten-day pass expired, but to that she also said yes. This time her mother didn't object.

Upon hearing the unusual news of a hospital-room wedding, the nursing staff hurriedly helped to get it organized. They borrowed flowers from other patients to make Shirley's room look less sterile. Agnes went downtown to buy her sister a wedding outfit, which would now have to be a nightgown and matching bed jacket instead of the billowing organza wedding gown of which Shirley had been dreaming. Anna would contact the minister at their church and ask him to perform the ceremony. She wasn't prepared when he said no.

The minister, being emotionally removed from the situation, couldn't imagine that Jim would really stand by a cripple. How in good conscience could he marry them? He thought, "What man, especially a healthy, young, attractive nineteen-year-old, would stay in a long-term union with a woman who would always be bed-bound with half her body unable to feel or move?" When Jim heard about the minister's refusal, he pleaded with him to reconsider. Jim knew it meant the world to Shirley, and, without realizing it, he was already fighting for her happiness. The minister saw infinite love in Jim's eyes. It was pure and from the center of his soul. Although the decision went against his pastoral intuition, the minister reluctantly agreed to perform the ceremony. It was not the wedding they had planned. It was even more beautiful because of the tried and true commitment that filled their hearts that day—February 5, 1953.

Like most grooms, Jim had been nervous, but believed he was the luckiest man in the world to have married Shirley Ann Friday. Shirley had her own secret trepidations, but knew that love would see them through. Their ceremony was resplendent and uniquely represented the marriage vows, especially "for better or worse."

As for their honeymoon, it would not be a drive to Omaha after all, and their wedding night would not be the romantic consummation about which they had fantasized. Instead, it was spent in a twin-size hospital bed, lying together utterly still at a forty-five-degree angle, with monitors constantly beeping. Jim did put a "Do Not Disturb" sign on the door, granting Shirley's wish, and, to their surprise, the doctors and nurses gave them one night of privacy to ponder their future. They couldn't have known then what a future it would be.

The first couple of years were committed to Shirley's grueling rehabilitation program. Just as she said she would, Shirley willed herself to sit up, despite the metal plate that lay against her spine. This allowed her to use a wheelchair and, at last, gave her freedom, though society didn't make mobility easy. Curbs made her wheels useless, narrow doorways prevented her chair's entry, and small bath-room stalls made it impossible to be away from home for too long. This didn't deter the Swansons. Jim would scoop up Shirley from her wheelchair and carry her into public restrooms, announcing on his way in that "a man is in the room." He lifted her chair over curbs and thresholds, and he even rigged a motorcycle handle bar and piano wire to the brake and gas pedals of the car, so she could drive. Out of necessity, Shirley began to speak up for herself and, in the process, for all other people with disabilities, asking that they have equal access to public buildings and streets. Although her words fell mostly on deaf ears, an idea—rather, a calling—was blossoming in Shirley's spirit.

Time passed quickly as Jim and Shirley got on with the business of daily life. They didn't realize that they were quietly becoming unique role models for everyone who met them—especially those challenged by physical disabilities, those with a broken heart searching for love, those who had lost faith in God, and those who were angry at the cards that life had dealt them. Shirley always offered a sympathetic ear to share a burden, while Jim, through his own example, showed the rewards of selflessness.

Before they knew it, seven years of newlywed bliss had passed. Shirley longed for children and often spoke of her desire. Jim begged her not to think about it. The doctors told them that the stress of a pregnancy on Shirley's damaged internal organs would be enough to kill her. Jim knew he couldn't live without his precious wife, so, for him, children were out of the question. For Shirley, it wasn't a ques-tion at all—they would have children.

After enduring the heartbreak of many near-term miscarriages, Shirley gave birth to four children between 1960 and 1972. The preg-nancies were difficult, and the births had been quite unorthodox at that time, requiring the doctors to use only Novocain to perform the caesarean section operations. Despite Jim's apprehension, Shirley had her babies and Jim couldn't imagine life without them.

For the next couple of decades, Jim worked hard—usually two or three jobs at a time as a draftsman—in order to provide a good home for his family. He succeeded beautifully. From her wheelchair, Shirley kept their home pristine, and their children were well-behaved and happy. She cooked three-course meals every night, mostly from vegetables she grew in the backyard, and mealtime was always a joyful family reunion at the end of a busy day. With much pleasure, Shirley toted her girls to ballet lessons, her sons to Little League baseball, and the whole bunch of them to swim team practice. High school homecoming dances and proms followed, as well as dance team and majorette performances, which she and Jim never missed. They encouraged their sons' love of music, provided electric guitars, and paid for hours of music lessons. Their children grew up and eventually left home to pursue academic and life goals that had been inspired by their parents' own glowing example. They came back, though, to celebrate their parents' fortieth wedding anniversary.

Friends and family gathered for the joyous occasion and enjoyed reminiscing about the good old days—the ups and downs and all the love in between. Jim and Shirley were touched that so many people wanted to share their special day, but were puzzled by a face in the crowd they didn't recognize. The woman stood quietly in a corner, avoiding eye contact or conversation. Reticently, she approached Jim and Shirley and introduced herself. "You don't know me, but my father received an invitation to your party, and asked me to attend on his behalf." It turned out that she was the daughter of the minister who had married them. He was now bedridden in a nursing home, but wanted his daughter to deliver a note. The handwriting revealed his shaking hand, but his words were clear:

"I thought I was making a mistake when I agreed to marry the both of you, but I saw something in your eyes. Perhaps it was a window to your loving souls that moved me to go against my instincts as a minister. Officiating at your ceremony was one of the most beautiful experiences I ever had as a man of God. Your love is God's love made manifest, and I am honored to have been a witness to it. Thank you for allowing me to be a part of your profound union."

The anniversary was a milestone that signaled a new chapter in Jim and Shirley's life together. With an empty nest, Shirley began to focus on her other calling. She became a voice for people with

disabilities. Her work and achievements as an activist were acknowledged and admired by city and state officials alike. She also began
working at the Independent Living Center, spreading her Pollyanna
goodness and showing people how they could live full and rewarding
lives despite their disabilities. Her motto was "Everyone has a disability—ours are only more visible."

After government funds were withdrawn and the center was
forced to close, Shirley accepted a position at the Veterans Adminis-
tration Hospital. She offered compassion and multifaceted assistance
to the veterans that had long been forgotten by our government.
However, on an ordinary autumn workday, Shirley, who never missed
a day of work, wasn't at her desk.

After having forced herself to go to the office the day before
despite a soaring fever, debilitating nausea, and Jim's protests, Shirley
finally collapsed at home. Jim rushed his unconscious wife to the hospital, where they diagnosed her condition as a deadly staphylococ-
cal skin infection, the kind that is resistant to treatment and usually
kills within twenty-four hours. The doctors asked for Jim's permission
to administer an enormous dose of antibiotics. They explained that
if he refused, Shirley would die. If he agreed, the infection would,
hopefully, be halted, thereby saving her life; but, at the very least, her
kidneys would shut down from the incredible amount of drugs puls-
ing through her veins. It was a selfish decision, but Jim couldn't live
without his Shirley, so he gave permission. She survived, but would
have to endure ten years, off and on, of dreadful dialysis. There came
a day, though, when even dialysis couldn't completely remove the
toxins from Shirley's blood.

She spent the last eight months of her life in the hospital. Jim
never left her side and even quit his job in order to spend every last
second with her. Our family tried to accept the inevitable, but we
never did. We didn't talk about death or the afterlife, we didn't plan
for a funeral, and we didn't say our goodbyes. We couldn't, until the
flat line on the heart monitor gave us only a few seconds to say all we
had wanted to say for the 244 days prior.

Shirley was gone. She was only sixty-three years old. As word
spread through our family and friends, the question on everyone's
mind was, How will Jim survive without Shirley?

It's odd, but in the chaos that followed her death, I remembered
a book I read when I was a kid. It was about a dog that lay on his
master's grave and couldn't be lured away with food, water, or kind-

ness. He just lay there until he died of a broken heart. I thought the same thing would happen to my dad, but it didn't.

Jim thrust himself into caring for his grown children, seeing them through the grief of losing a parent. He bravely greeted an endless stream of mourning visitors and personally answered every condolence letter.

On rare occasions, Jim admitted that grief "filled his heart and soul," making him ache mercilessly from the inside out. Somehow he managed to wake each day, remembering to breathe and putting one foot in front of the other, until yet another day had passed. Days turned into months, and before he knew it five years had passed. He was sure about one thing: that there wasn't any truth to the saying "Time heals all wounds." He confided in his children that he wished he could at least visit with his darling in his dreams, but depression-induced insomnia prevented such a reunion. He hoped he would sense her spirit around him, but felt nothing. He had all but given up in what others call afterlife communication until he met Linda Drake.

Jim became acquainted with Linda after receiving a gift certificate for his seventy-second birthday that granted him a one-hour reading with the well-known psychic. He was afraid to get his hopes up, but couldn't help being excited at the possibility of connecting with his one and only true love. Jim wasn't disappointed.

For the first time since her death, he heard Shirley's voice. Of course, it was coming through Linda, but the words were all Shirley's. They reflected the wit she possessed while she was here and recounted some of the sweet memories that were only theirs. There was no doubt in Jim's mind that it was, indeed, his sweetheart speaking to him from beyond the grave.

With exultation in her voice, Shirley began by telling Jim, "I love you, I love you! These words I said so often when I was with you, and even now they cannot begin to describe the depth and enormity of my love for you." Shirley then said to Linda, "This man is grand! He never failed me. When I was sick, he was so good to me. We had a great love and a great life.

"It wasn't always easy, but we were always there for each other. And . . ." Linda tried to catch her breath.

She told Shirley to please slow down, that she wasn't able to repeat everything so quickly, and they had plenty of time to talk. Linda chuckled and told Jim that she could see Shirley talking a mile a minute. Shirley quipped, "I've waited a long time for him to hear my words. There are others here with me, his mother and his Uncle Gene, but I have much to say first." Jim laughed out loud, knowing that is exactly what she would have said if she had been there. Linda paused to explain that spirits carry their personalities with them and really are the same as when they were here. She asked, "Was your wife one to tell it like it is?" "Oh, yes," Jim said, with much melancholy. "That's what I loved about her."

Shirley interrupted their conversation and said to Linda, "Tell him that I've never left him. When I first crossed over, many loved ones greeted me. There was no more pain, only joy and love. Now, I've returned to Jim. I walk beside him always. I sleep next to him every night and caress his head. I sat beside him when the tears rolled down his face and when he held them back. Tell him that I will stay with him until he is ready to cross. Then, we will dance across the rainbow bridge together."

Jim was obviously moved by her comments. His voice cracked as he told Linda that he desperately wished he could feel his wife next to him. Shirley impetuously said, "Tell him the signs!" Linda revealed that spirits use common ways to show us they are here, like flickering the lights, moving an object off a shelf, or turning the radio or television on or off. Jim softly gasped and said, "That happens to my TV all the time. When I'm in bed and almost asleep, the TV comes on. I just thought it was a power surge or a cable problem." Linda said that it was Shirley and to keep looking for the subtle signs of presence.

Then, there was a long silence. Linda sighed heavily, but was smiling. Jim didn't understand, until Linda told them that she could feel the love between them, and it filled her with absolute joy. Jim was eager to tell her about their love. "We had something special. I mean, I love my children, but that is nothing compared to how much I loved Shirley." "I know," she said. "Your love is indescribably beautiful." A vision of Shirley twirling around the room wearing a smile that radiated bliss refocused Linda's attention.

She told Jim what she was seeing. He closed his eyes and tried to imagine it. With childlike excitement, Shirley told Jim," You should see my new body. It's strong and my legs are beautiful." Suddenly, she sounded like a flirting teenager. He said, "I liked the other body just fine, but I can understand why she is happy with a new one. Now she can dance." "Oh, I'm dancing all right," Shirley blurted out. "And when you cross over, we will dance together forever." Solemnly she added, "But, it's not your time yet."

Jim doubted that. His heart was failing. His body ached. He was so tired. He just wanted to go home to his sweetheart. Just like in life, for forty-six years, Shirley admonished him: "Now you listen to me, Jim Swanson. You have got to take care of yourself. You have much to do before your time is through. I can't take that medicine for you, and I can't call the doctor when you need help, so you've got to do what is right. Besides, who is going to take care of our family? Who is going to keep everybody in line?"

Linda giggled, realizing that she was like a fly on the wall watching a married couple pretend to quarrel.

"We never fussed, mind you," Jim conveyed to Linda. "We didn't always agree, but we never argued or raised our voices to each other." In this day and age, Linda found that hard to believe, but knew it was true. Shirley then took the opportunity to tell Jim that his greatest gift to his children was the love he had for their mother.

She said, "You taught them about love and commitment in a way no one else in the world could have. For that, I will be forever grateful." Humbly, as he had for forty-six years, Jim gave all the credit to his wife. "Shirley raised our kids practically by herself." Then, like they were having a private conversation, Shirley said, "Do you remember when you used to come home from work at 2 a.m., and I would be up cooking you dinner? Well, times like those, when I was caring for you and the kids, I was completely fulfilled. That was enough for me. I had a great life, a life full of meaning. I have no regrets."

Amazed, Linda realized that she was seeing glimpses of the extraordinary life of two people who, before the reading, had been strangers to her. She felt honored to be their line of communication. The reading continued for a bit longer. Initially, Jim had wondered what they would talk about for a whole hour, but realized the time had passed all too quickly. There was so much more to say.

After the reading, and for days afterward, Jim processed his emotions. He still misses his wife terribly; nothing will change that. But the heavy blanket of grief that has weighed him down for the past five years seems a bit lighter. Knowing that not only is Shirley at peace, but that she is jubilant in the afterlife, makes Jim truly happy. Maybe he just needed to know she was all right. It was a bonus to learn that she is still around him, taking care of him and loving him.

He finds himself smiling when the lights flicker, and he is surprised to hear his own voice talking toward the ceiling, where he imagines Shirley's spirit is hovering. Once again, he looks forward to lying in

bed at night. Before, it was emotionally excruciating to lie there without his wife, who had shared a bed with him for nearly five decades.
Now, he watches for any unusual rustling of the covers or an unsus-
pected touch to his head. Like Linda suggested, Jim pays attention to
the air around him, hoping that one day he will smell Shirley's sweet
scent or the smell of Avon's Skin So Soft, Shirley's favorite bath oil,
which she bathed in every night right before he came home from
his late-night job. Jim remembers that it was that aroma that greeted
him at the door first, telling him that romance was in the air. He's
surprised at how his senses have been heightened at the prospect of
visiting with his wife and feels infused with a new kind of strength to
go on.

Some people, especially skeptics, might not believe all this talk of
afterlife communication. Jim can imagine their argument about wish-
ful thinking and a lack of scientific proof, but it doesn't matter to
him. Just the other day a memory came to him while he was thinking
about life after death. He recalled a verse from the Bible: "Let those
that have ears hear." He always knew what that meant, even though
most people don't. Jesus was explaining that spiritual ears will always
recognize truth. He had recognized truth in his wife's words spoken
in Linda's voice.

At the beginning of each reading, Linda asks Jesus to guide her to
help and heal, especially those with grief-stricken hearts. Jim is grateful that the request was granted. New life has been breathed back
into him. His faith in everlasting life has been renewed and his belief
in a merciful God has been refreshed, and now he can get on with
the work he has to finish before crossing over the rainbow bridge
with his Shirley.

The story that Sherri has shared with us is one chapter from the book she
is writing about her parents' love and her mother's courage. I thank her
for sharing it with us.

chapter two

Death: Moving Forward on Your Soul's Journey

This chapter is based entirely on my experiences with spirits who have passed over and information I have received from Spirit. Accept the information that feels comfortable for you and release the rest. We are not all at the same place on our paths. Treasures all along our path wait for us to discover them when we are ready. That is what makes life an adventure.

Early on in this adventure of my life, I was given this message from Spirit:

> Death is a gift from God. It is God's reward to us for fulfilling our life purpose. Through death we are allowed to return home to God's unconditional love. His love heals all the wounds of our life, and he rewards us for meeting the challenges of our life purpose.

God was with us when we designed what our lives would hold. God saw the ambition within us as we chose to heal the karma of our many lifetimes. He surrounded us with his angels and guides to support us through these challenges. The importance of our life purpose is not determined by the length of our life. Whether our life lasts for ninety-nine years or less than one hour, we have a life purpose. When that purpose is fulfilled, we are rewarded as God sends his special angels to hold our hands when we choose to come home.

For most of the people with whom I talk about death, it is not the afterlife they fear, but the actual death and leaving loved ones behind. This is understandable. But, in talking with those who have already crossed over, I always receive the same message: they were not alone at their time of death. An angel or a family member was sent to assist them in their crossing, and a powerful loving energy was present, an energy so beautiful that they could not describe it. I have waited in hospital rooms, watching as angels and loved ones in spirit gathered, excitedly anticipating the event of their loved one's crossing. They see the process as their loved one coming home. I am often told, by those in spirit, of the angel that pulled them out of the car just before the impact, preventing them from suffering the pain of the accident. I have had those in spirit tell me about standing beside the bed and watching as their physical body released its last breath of life, ending the physical struggle. Those in spirit rarely talk about trauma when referring to their physical death. Instead, they talk of the instant joy and overwhelming love that greeted them in a blink of an eye. They sometimes talk about the beautiful tunnel of light that they were drawn into. I am told that this is the doorway to God, and that his love is welcoming them home.

I have witnessed the consciousness of the soul, as it appeared like a stream of smoke leaving the human body at the exact time of death. At this point, the person officially releases the physical density of their human body and gains the freedom of spirit. Time on the other side is very different from time here. There is no perception of time when we cross over. We are welcomed home by our loved ones already in spirit. Then there is a period of transition. I am told that our spirits can make the choice of staying in the place of unconditional love that God provides for us, or they can do a quick transitional healing. This transitional healing is just enough to enable them to return to us in spirit form in order to assist us with our healing process. If this is the choice they make, they will actually slow down their own soul's journey, using their energy to hold a space on this earthly plane while they complete an obligation to someone they have left behind. When a loved one chooses to return in spirit to assist *us* in healing our grief, you can imagine the sacrifice they have made, as their soul's journey has been put on hold.

As our consciousness advances in our spiritual awareness, the veil between those living in body and those in spirit form is becoming increasingly thin. Those in spirit want us to understand more about their existence. One beautiful soul in spirit, whose earthly name was Bob, took the time to explain to me what life was like on the other side. He said, "It is like being able to breathe in the most beautiful feeling of love with every breath." You have to admit, it sounds delightful!

I have worked with people in all stages of life, preparing them for their transition. Whether this transition is to come in one hour or many years in their future, we are all working our way toward death. Many hold the traditional perception of death as the end of life, when actually it is only the end of one phase of our life and the beginning of a new one. Remember how excited you were when you turned eighteen years old? You were transitioning from adolescence to adulthood. You were graduating to a new stage of life that represented great freedom and a wonderful new adventure for you. Try looking at death in exactly the same way. Death brings a freedom that allows us to ride on the wings of angels. One of my clients, now in spirit, gave me that illustration of death after she left.

Spirit likens our soul's journey to how we experience our earthly days. As the sun rises, life begins, bringing new beginnings. As we start each day, it may hold excitement, happiness, and joy, or it may hold challenges of illness, sadness, and grief. These are all experiences that allow us to grow, to make our own choices, and to take control of our lives. You can see the opportunities and challenges of your life from any perspective you choose. As the sun sets, there is the wonder and beauty of what we have completed in that day or that lifetime. God gives us beautiful sunsets as a sign of completion to remind us that death is our breathtaking reward for all that we accomplished in that one day or that one lifetime.

Since I was given the gift of communicating with those who have crossed over, I have been tremendously enlightened about the process of death. The belief that most of us grew up with is that death is the end, the end of our life, the end of our existence; but I have found that to be far from the truth. An important part was left out: death is only the end of our existence in this particular human body, the end of *one* chapter in our life. The complete journey of our soul's existence is contained in a big book in God's library. This book holds the knowledge and experiences of each lifetime, and we continue to add to it. That same knowledge of our soul's existence is held within our spiritual DNA.

I often have souls in spirit form come to me asking that I explain to their loved ones how death works. This is difficult for me, since I have not experienced the complete process myself, so I have always left it up to Spirit to give me the words, as I will now:

We realize that for some, having a better understanding of death is very comforting. This is what we desire for you. When it is your time to cross the threshold of death, it happens in the blink of an eye. For some, there is a tunnel of light, and for others, just a bright light that they pass through at the time the soul leaves the body for the last time. It's what exists on the other side that is important. There is a great energy of love that envelops your spirit, welcoming you home. This involves a heartfelt reunion with your soul group, including your family, friends, and loved ones. Death is not the end of life for you. For a period of time, you will no longer be in the density of a human body, but the same spirit that occupied that body remains alive. There is a life force energy that is connected to every spirit; that energy continues to exist. Your spirit, or soul, as it is frequently referred to, has the choice to return to earth in spirit form for a limited time to remain among your loved ones. This often happens if you feel a great responsibility to loved ones left behind. Sometimes you may feel that you have not finished what you came to do in this lifetime, so you return to supervise its completion. The soul in spirit has the ability to travel, allowing its energy to be in many places at once, if necessary.

From a human perspective, I enjoy knowing that at any time we can call on our loved ones in spirit and they will come to be with us, as they continue to interact with us even in their spirit form. They are especially close to us when we near our own death. We may not hear them or see them, but we must trust that they will be there for us, just as we trust that God will not abandon us. They often tell me how they enjoy talking with us. Even though we are seldom able to hear their voices, they listen to us. If we still ourselves long enough, we can learn to feel their energy. Their energy can affect electrical energy, causing the lights to flicker or go off. As their energy becomes stronger, they are able to move things, all in an effort to get our attention. They can come to us in our dreams to give us messages, or we may awaken during the night to see them standing by the bed. Pennies are left for us, and songs are played for us. Those in spirit want us to be reminded of them, to know they haven't left us. All of these occurrences are common, but we are usually too busy rushing through our lives to notice them, or we are not ready to see them. Our loved ones in spirit delight in joining family celebrations, just as we do. We simply need to pay attention to the signs of their presence that they give us.

Cheryn came to me, as most of my clients do, through word of mouth. As Cheryn describes her experience, you will see how important it was for her to have that connection with her daughter, who had died. Knowing that her daughter was still with her gave her the strength to begin healing the pain, grief, and loneliness of her loss.

> I had heard of Linda through a woman who worked for the same company that I did. This woman and I worked independently at our own homes, and I had met her only once and felt immediately that we had a connection. On the phone, we shared memories about our daughters, who both had died, and shared feelings about the difficulty of living without them. She called one day to give me a telephone number that had been passed on to her by her friend in Austin. She told me about Linda and her ability to connect people with their loved ones who had died. I called Linda and made an appointment, giving her just my name. When I showed up for the appointment, Linda greeted me, we walked into her office, and she said, "You're here to meet with your daughter. She's right behind you."
>
> From there our session continued with Linda validating many, many things for me. She talked about instances in my daughter's life that she could not have known without help from God and my daughter. I broke down when Linda said she was unwrapping candy—butterscotch candy. My dad had always greeted Christy with a little piece of butterscotch candy from his pocket. Linda talked about milestones in my daughter's life, and I came to the conclusion that Linda has a divine gift to help those of us here to carry on until we cross over and join our loved ones. I had experienced visits from Christy before I met Linda, but that visit was the step I needed on my road to recovery. I am convinced our spirit does live on and that our transition into the next place is just that—a transition. I now understand and accept the grace of God.

Thank you, Cheryn, for sharing your experience with us.

For those in spirit with whom I have worked, their human personality often remains with them after they pass. If they held negativity prior to death, I usually see that released from them, as they have an understanding of the whole picture that we do not have. They may comment about the challenges of their previous personality traits, but it is difficult for them to hold the negativity of their human existence. They evidently keep their sense of humor, as they often share it with me. These souls are very aware of the karma they created, and have a goal of trying to heal what they can from the other side. That is why they often do what they can to bring their loved ones to healers such as myself.

We are awakened to the realization that our loved ones in spirit continue to interact with us. The greatest blessing that God has given us is our communication with God through prayer. God hears our every word, and it is important for us to pray for our deceased loved one to have a blessed journey as their soul moves along its path. Our loved ones in spirit often pray for us, as they are totally aware of the challenges we are experiencing as we continue our journey here on earth. With the veil becoming thinner, I hope the time is near for all of us to be able to reach through to hear the words and feel the embrace of our loved ones in spirit.

Souls in spirit do not always remain on earth. Many return for a short period, but few of them stay for long periods of time. If they are finished with their life here, they are ready to join their loved ones on the other side. They can return as often as they choose, continually giving support and messages to their loved ones in body.

After the transition period, the human spirit embraces the new beginning. There are decisions to be made and work to be done. We start with a time of rest and healing of any trauma experienced in the most recent life. Then follows another transition, as the spirit adjusts to its new form and is reminded of how things work there. Heaven, as many of us refer to it, is not a place for slacking off. It is like a fine-tuned corporation with many jobs to be done, just as we have here on earth. As the soul goes through the healing process, it reviews the life it has just left, noting accomplishments as well as failures.

By accomplishments, I do not mean what job was held or how big the house was, or what kind of car was driven. Rather, I mean the important things in life: What karma did you heal? Whose life did you touch in a positive way? What examples did you set by showing love and kindness? In going through the healing process, the soul observes its life, seeing the karma created and the karma healed. The soul evaluates the job it did in this life, and how well it accomplished its life plan. Remember that the life plan was the purpose of that lifetime.

The Footprints of Our Lives

- Are there deep footprints, as you carried your burdens along with the burdens of others, making it easy for people to follow the example of your path?

- Did your footprints create a circle of love embracing all those in need into its strength and support?
- Did your footprints climb to the top of the mountain, creating a path of encouragement for others to follow?
- Did your footprints leave the imprint of marching boots, as you bravely served your country?
- Did your footprints have a circle of little ones around them, as you left the imprint of your words on their hearts?
- Did your footprints walk the extra mile to help poor souls in need?
- Did your footprints show signs of blood and blisters, as you walked that long hard road of life, enduring and conquering the challenges of your life purpose?
- Did your footprints leave only a shadow of the unfulfilled dreams of what you could have accomplished?

Of course, the question that each of us must ask is: When I am gone, what footprints will I leave behind?

As I said, there are many jobs to be done on the other side. Each soul is given a job that fits its talents or its needs. Those in spirit have come to me, telling about the jobs they chose on the other side. Some delight in being greeters (like the ones we have at Wal-Mart), some are guides who help the new ones find their way, and others become planners, to help new arrivals plan their lives when they are ready to return in body. The old souls are teachers, helping the new souls understand their purpose. Then there are the organizers who keep things moving smoothly; we couldn't do without them.

One client came back after his death to brag that he had gotten a job working with the souls that had committed suicide, since they need a lot of healing work and he had the understanding and compassion they needed. He felt he was perfect for the job. Another one of my clients, whom I had grown to love dearly, excitedly returned after his death with the message that he had finished his procession of lives and no longer had to return. What a celebration he was having! Knowing all that he had given to others in this life, I understood. I quickly put in my request for him to be my spirit guide in my next lifetime.

As your soul progresses along its path, the assignments will change. At some point, the spirit is ready to begin planning for a return into the next life. This may occur in weeks, months, years, or even centuries, since there is no measurement of time there. The world to which spirit beings transition is unlike anything we can imagine here.

Through my interaction with clients, I am presented with many questions. Here is one I am often asked: When we enter heaven, are the souls of good people mixed in with the dark souls of murderers?

These are Spirit's words:

> In human form, the darkness lives within all of you. You make a conscious choice as to what energy you will give the darkness. With karma, there is always payback for that which is created. Do not stand in judgment, as this empowers the darkness within you. Stand in forgiveness, for the burden of karma that those in the darkness must carry is great.
>
> You are all loved unconditionally by God, but the choices you make during your lifetimes on earth determine the karma you create. This karma holds a vibration. The karma created by the negative energy of crimes against humanity is bonded to that soul; this negative energy decreases the soul's spiritual vibration. When the human body dies and the soul is released, it goes through the same transition of death, only it is taken to a level separate from others of a higher spiritual vibration. That soul is given the opportunity for additional healing and atonement for its actions. The soul created the karma; only through the healing of the karma in the next lifetime will the soul be released from its journey.

As we discussed in chapter 1, karma is an energy that you have the choice of creating. Whatever energy you create and express, positive or negative, will come back to you in that same way. This energy can come back to you in the same lifetime in which it was created, with that same person, or it can be carried throughout many lifetimes. When the karmic experience comes back around to you, it comes with an opportunity to heal it, and that choice is yours.

Every action has an energy connected to it, and that creates karma. For example, when you carry judgment in your heart for a person or race of people, that judgment will always come back to you. You will be put in a position to suffer that same judgment. If it is projected with a negative intention, it will come back just as painfully or destructively. This is God's way of allowing us to learn our lessons. One such lesson is to treat others as you would want to be treated. God will not judge us, but he will allow us to learn through karma. Even a child learns karma. If a child hits another child and that child hits him back harder, he learns about karma very quickly; but if they hug each other and there is forgiveness, they learn how to heal karma. Do not despair if negativity comes your way. Just know that you are clearing karma that you had previously created.

Spirit tells me that any time we sincerely ask in prayer for blessings for someone, it produces love and is returned tenfold.

Words of Advice from the Other Side

What advice would those who have passed over give to us in this realm? Here are some of the messages I have heard:

- Live each day to the fullest, with no regrets.
- Express your love daily. It's the most important thing you have to give.
- Love and appreciate everything life gives you, both challenges and celebrations.
- Find joy in every day. Eat chocolate and ice cream.
- Forgiveness is a treasure for both involved, but anger creates a pain that destroys love.
- Your life is your choice. Don't gripe about it—change it!
- Not everyone will love you. Treasure those who do.
- Don't miss an opportunity to share your hugs.
- Life is full of pain. Heal all wounds now, not someday, as someday may not come.
- And my favorite is: Death is like getting a new box of crayons and a big fat coloring book in which to create the new beginnings of your next life.

Death, for those spirits crossing over, is a celebration. However, since those in spirit are able to see our grief and feel the pain of our experience, many in spirit return quickly following their death, hoping to assist their loved ones through the trauma of the funeral and the grieving process. Some in spirit stay for a short time, while others stay for many years.

Spirit brings us opportunities in many forms to help us heal our grief; our readiness to heal is our choice. In this next case, Laura felt driven to find answers, as she was ready to begin her healing path.

I met Linda Drake at my first psychic fair, shortly after the death of my mother and beloved brother. I had never been to a psychic fair before and was brought up in a strict Catholic family where such things as after-death communication were *never* spoken of.

It was about four months after their deaths, and I was desperately searching for affirmation that they were still with me. I had become a follower of the New Age movement about a year before their passing, so I was totally open to whatever Spirit had in mind for me.

I awoke around 5 a.m. that Saturday morning, nervous and anxious to attend the fair. I was to meet a good friend of mine there, which soothed my anxiety quite a bit. I got there early, about thirty minutes before the fair was to start. After consuming all of the coffee I am famous for drinking, I immediately headed for the nearest ladies room. As soon as I entered, I noticed a very attractive woman with an incredible aura about her . . . a beautiful woman with dark hair and an angel pendant that caught my eye. As we each washed our hands, we exchanged pleasantries and I immediately felt so comfortable with the whole thing. I gave it no more thought and headed for the room to attend what would be the first of many psychic fairs that I would attend.

I met with my friend and her mom, and we anxiously anticipated what would happen to us. It was wonderful, crystals and books everywhere and lots of people doing different types of psychic work all around the room. The energy was very high, and the chatter of voices could be heard throughout the crowded room. I nervously walked around, praying and hoping for a sign as to who was the one I should seek a reading with. And who do you think I saw doing readings at a table at the front of the room? The same beautiful woman I had encountered in the ladies room only minutes earlier. I knew she was the right one and eagerly signed up for my reading.

I nervously waited my turn, and when I finally received my reading, it was so amazing. She remembered me from the ladies room and put me at ease, as my hands were shaking and I was teary-eyed. The first card I drew was the "death" card. Linda immediately picked up on the fact that it was my mother who had recently died. She assured me that she was still with me and in a *big* way. She said that my mom was with me now helping me heal. She then picked up on an even bigger issue . . . the fact that my best friend, one of the dearest souls in my life, my brother Rick, had passed away only twenty days after Mom. I was devastated, heartbroken, and unable to move forward. Not only had I lost my mom, but my best friend, Rick, had left me too. Through communicating with them, Linda assured me that they were both still with me, watching over me, and helping me from the other side. She explained to me how their deaths would be the vehicle for me to learn and experience this part of my life. They explained that it was their path to leave together at this time and how losing them would assist in opening me up to my spiritual path. Their deaths had in fact opened me up to a whole new chapter of my life. They were speaking through Linda to let me know they were both with me and still guiding me from the other side. They had not left me; they were very much a part of my life, just from the other side now, and they were to help me with the plan I had agreed to earlier on the other side with them. Both my mom and brother were excited about continuing to help me heal my grief and move forward with my life, as I have greater things to do and be, here in this life-time. Linda gave me messages from them that only they would have known, giving me confirmation that they were actually there for me. I needed their words to give me the strength to heal my loss.

My mother continues to guide me through this life, helping me work on lessons I have come to learn. I know she guided me to Linda so that she could give me clarification on some of the most important issues of my life. Each time I see Linda, she tells me things that only my family could know and pass along to me. Linda is their way of getting their information through to me.

I hope you can understand, through this letter, how our loved ones in spirit will guide us to the right place and the right person to assist us in our healing process, just as Laura's mother did.

chapter three

Grief: Understanding It and Healing It

The Different Personality Types
and How We Grieve

Before I can begin explaining about grief, you must first understand how humanity is made up of different types of people. Some of us are emotional, some of us are unemotional/logical, and some of us are a combination/balanced. Through our experiences we are all striving to reach that place of balance. We each grieve according to our personality type. Grief is unique to each survivor, with no one person experiencing it in the same manner as another.

The first type of personality is the emotional type. These people are truly in touch with every emotion they have. They feel their emotions with all of their senses, they express their emotions freely, and their lives are guided by their own emotional needs as well as their need to care for others. These are the healers and caretakers of humanity, constantly striving to fulfill the physical and emotional needs of everyone.

The downside for this personality type is that sometimes they become so wrapped up in their emotions that they fail to see the reality of the situation, angering the logical people around them.

The second type of personality is the logical type. These people are very analytical; life for them is not about emotion. Things are either black or white for them—there is no gray. They think that if something is broke, don't whine about it—fix it. These people are often seen as the strength and the backbone of humanity. Logical people take pride in self-discipline and structure, and providing personal or national security is often an achievement they relish. Their emotions are always in check, as they see the inability to control emotions as a sign of weakness; thus, they have difficulty understanding or being sensitive to the emotional needs of others.

The downside of this type of personality is that they rarely allow themselves to get in touch with their own emotions. Their logical attitude can anger emotional people, since they can appear cold and uncaring. It is not that they do not have emotions; it is that their emotions are controlled so tightly they are not comfortable experiencing them, unlike the emotional types, who readily express all of their emotions. When logical personalities do express their emotions, it is often through an explosive loss of temper, and they often have a bad temper when pushed too far. Referring to this type of personality as logical does not mean that their thinking is always logical. What is logical to one person may seem irrational to another. It is a matter of perception. They do not allow their emotions to interfere with their thought process. They express themselves as thinking, not feeling.

Your personality type is also influenced by the people responsible for your upbringing. In trying to earn love and respect, we model ourselves after the people with the most influence on our lives.

Within each person is the ability to function using both of these personality types, but usually we find ourselves in our comfort zone of exhibiting our dominant personality type.

Your dominant personality type correlates with your chosen life path issues. As you heal the karma of those issues, you will often see your dominant personality type blend into the recessive traits, creating the balanced personality. This is why it is important that we learn from our experiences.

This third personality type, the combined, or balanced, personality, is usually created through the knowledge that the person has gained by the karma healed through their life experiences. This personality operates using both concepts of emotion and logic. They have basically learned to function in both worlds and to use the best qualities of both personality types to survive. This type of person has an emotional, caring attitude, striving to meet the needs of others, but in a very organized, logical way. They may not understand those emotional needs, but they understand that having those needs met is important to others. The balanced personality may have strong basic traits of either personality type, utilizing the knowledge they have gained for the sake of all. The balanced type of person may accept that they have emotions and may occasionally communicate about them, but only when logic dictates that it is necessary. At times the pendulum can swing either way, utilizing both traits.

The downside for the balanced personality is that everyone comes to this person for help. Whether their problem is emotional or logical, people expect this person to have the answer, as they sense that the person can see the situation from both perspectives.

Please note that these personality traits are not limited to either gender.

We hope you will not be offended or insulted by any of the descriptions or definitions we have used. We are not being judgmental, as we are only trying to demonstrate for you where misunderstandings can occur, as we each experience situations from different perspectives. Our first experience with grief may have been as a child. At a young age, we may not have understood the emotions created by the loss of a loved one, a pet, or a friendship as grief, but we felt the emotional pain and emptiness of our loss. As a result of our losses, both big and small, we are learning about and being prepared for future losses. These experiences teach us about life, death, and the emotion of grief.

It is important to recognize the different personality types to better understand how each may deal with grief in their own way. Grief is the process of letting go of someone or something that is very dear to you. The grieving process is like trying to heal a tear that has been ripped open in your heart. Grief is often an emotion attached to the transition of death, but it is not always limited to death; it is the process of healing a loss in your life. The grief can involve losing a person, an animal, a relationship, or a job, leaving a painfully empty place within us. We can apply any of these analogies to your loss. Grief is a very personal thing, as we all approach our loss in a different way. Some describe their grieving experience like being on a roller coaster, since they experience one emotion after another, frequently lasting months or even years.

Some people hold all of their emotions inside, believing they have to be strong at that time for one reason or another. They try to make themselves numb to the pain. More often than not, they are only postponing healing the emotions of grief.

If they are the emotional type, it won't take long before they eventually fall apart. This is only natural for them because of their emotional side. Trying to suppress it is like trying to stop a volcano; eventually it will erupt, spewing emotions everywhere, like hot lava, ash, and smoke.

For the emotional person, the very act of crying is one of many valuable healing tools. It is okay to fall apart and be emotional. You are not the nursery rhyme character Humpty Dumpty—you *can* put yourself back together again. For you, it is only natural to let your emotions flow. Your family history or culture may have taught you that you have to be strong, holding back your emotions, but you have to find a way of grieving that is right for you. The loss of a loved one can be a devastating and traumatic event in your life, whether the loved one is a child, parent, spouse, friend, or family pet. The emotions can run the full range from feeling like you've had a kick in the stomach that knocks the breath out of you, to a guilt-ridden sense of relief that your loved one is no longer suffering. From one extreme to another, grief must still be dealt with and resolved in your own unique way.

When you are suffering the pain of grief, this is the time to reach out to others and allow them to help you. Surrounding yourself with loving, nurturing family and friends will be your greatest tool for healing. You need to talk, reminiscing about your life with your loved one and discussing your thoughts, feelings, and needs. Give yourself permission to heal, to smile, to enjoy life again, and eventually you will find yourself laughing out loud, much to your surprise. Give yourself time and you will gradually reenter the flow of life.

With an unexpected death, as with other losses, it is not unusual to revisit the depths of grief about six months following the loss. Just about the time you think you have your emotions under control, the painful memories come flooding back. This may come in the form of dreams in which you are reliving the loss, but you can't stop it. This may take you back to that feeling of helplessness. Remember the healing steps that got you back into the flow of life, and start that journey again.

Memories from the past will always bring up your feelings of grief. Your loved ones do not want to be forgotten, but they prefer that you remember all of the joyful memories of their life rather than the painful ones of their death. Holidays and special days can be especially painful. Make an effort to change up the usual traditions, but don't be alone. Surround yourself with friends or family who will understand what you are going through. If friends and family are not accessible, search for a place to do volunteer work, and occupy your hands and mind by helping others. There are many great volunteer organizations that could use an extra pair of hands around the holidays, and helping others soothes the heart. Do it in memory of your loved ones. Do not allow yourself to fall into the depths of depression when you are truly needed by so many. If you find you cannot overcome the depression during these difficult times, don't be embarrassed to go to your physician for medication to help you. Contact your minister or priest, and reach out for help by letting someone know what is going on with you.

You know you are on your healing path when you think of your deceased loved one and the previous tears are replaced with a smile, as you remember all of the wonderful memories you hold in your heart.

Grief Is Like a Burning Building . . .

This is how one of my clients explained grief to me: it is like awakening to find yourself in a burning building. The horror in the situation throws you into a state of fear, shock, and confusion. You try to remember what others have told you about how to handle a situation like this. Your first instinct is to put out the fire (to take control of the emotions), and when you realize you can't stop the situation, you want to run, to try to escape, but the smoke (emotion) is too thick; it is like a fog you can't move through. In a state of confusion, you drop to the floor and crawl through the darkness (fog of emotions), and as you inch your way forward, you are praying to find the exit around the next corner, but there seems to be a never-ending maze of hallways (emotions to experience). You keep trying to stand up to scream for help, but each time you do, the toxins (pain) choke back the words. You begin to fear you will never emerge from this frightening maze of darkness (unending fog of emotions). After what seems to be an eternity, you see a window of daylight. You question yourself: Am I imagining this, or is the clearing of the smoke (fog of emotions) real? Have I survived the devastation of my situation (having clarity and control of emotions)? To your relief, help has arrived (family and friends). They had been there all along, but you were so deep in your maze of smoke that they couldn't reach you. You struggle back into the world, remembering what it feels like to breathe fresh air. You have lived through the devastating ordeal (grief), and you will survive. You will carry the horrifying memories of the experience for the rest of your life, but you had the strength to survive and go on with your life. Your joyful memories of life prior to this experience will become your strength, enabling you to embrace your life and fulfill your life purpose.

Once you have experienced the loss of a loved one, and sometimes even before the actual passing, you begin to experience the many different stages of grief.

The Webster Dictionary defines grief as "an intense emotional suffering caused by loss, disaster, misfortune, acute and deep sorrow." We usually identify grief as an emotion that is associated with the death of a friend or loved one, but there are many other types of loss that can cause us to experience grief. Our loss can involve a friendship, a pet, a marriage, a relationship, a job, or anything that we feel holds great importance in our lives. The depth of attachment to the loss will determine the intensity of our grief. When the loss is unexpected or tragic, we are caught off guard and feel as though we have no control over our grief or how we are experiencing it. We talk about the process of grieving as having different stages, but it is unique to everyone, and we each experience it in different ways and for different lengths of time. Each loss we encounter in our lives gives us the experience and strength to deal with the next. New losses frequently give us the opportunity to process the grief of a previous loss. Your grief over the loss of a loved one will never completely go away, but as you process your grief, the emotions will diminish and no longer be as raw and painful.

Grief involves the process of mourning and frequently carries an overwhelming feeling of sadness with it. In moving through the mourning process, we learn to live again, without the presence of that special something or someone in our lives.

The Stages of Grief

April 3, 2009
still have all of these
Aug. 1 2012

The stages of grief are as follows:

1. Shock, numbness, disbelief, and denial.
2. Feeling the pain by accepting the reality of your loss.
3. Despair and disorganization.
4. Need to talk about the deceased person, your loss, and your emotions.
5. Wading through the flood of disconnected emotions of guilt, anger, and judgment, as you feel helpless in the situation.
6. Missing and longing for the lost person or object.
7. Adjusting to the environment without the loved one.
8. Redefining who you are without that person or thing as part of your life.
9. Learning to reenter the flow of life.

All of these stages may be accompanied by tears. Use them to cleanse yourself of the pain of your loss. You may experience all or some of these stages, or your stages of grief may be completely different. If you find yourself stuck experiencing one stage for an extended amount of time, you may be unable to move forward without help. You may find it necessary to seek professional grief counseling.

To heal, it is often necessary to allow yourself to feel and express your deepest emotions. Communication is a tool; whether these emotions are of overwhelming sadness about the loss, or the fear of being alone, or the anger of abandonment, they all need to be acknowledged and expressed. This is a part of the healing that is achieved throughout the grieving process. Don't be timid! Emotional people benefit greatly from the caring and comfort of other emotional people. As the one left behind, this is your time to reach out and accept the love and nurturing of others to aid you in your healing process. You need to talk, repeating your stories over and over. Find an emotional type of person to help you with this, as they love to listen.

Logical people frequently approach death from a different perspective. For them, the death of a loved one is accepted with little or no emotion. I am not saying the loss is not as devastating to the logical person or that they do not deeply feel the loss; it is just felt in a different way, not in an outwardly emotional way. They process within themselves without verbalization, often having difficulty understanding the emotions of others. These are usually the people who hold everything together while the rest of us fall apart. They logically accept the loss and staunchly move forward with their lives. There is nothing wrong with this type of acceptance of death, as it is the only way that the logical personality can deal with their loss. This may work fine for them for a while, except that occasionally there is a crying child within them that needs to experience the emotional healing process, as foreign as it may feel to the adult.

For most of us, no matter which personality type we are, it is necessary to go through a grieving process of some sort.

Grief counseling can be very helpful and sometimes necessary to assist you through your healing process. You can choose from individual counseling or group counseling, depending on which you are most comfortable with. The grieving child within us can hide so very well that we often do not discover the child's emotions for many years. For some, this denial only works until their emotions begin erupting in unexplainable ways. An emotional person can accept these emotions, but a logical person has great difficulty in analyzing the situation. This unprocessed grief can manifest as phases of anger, anxiety, depression, fear, isolation, or obsession. Any one of these, when taken to the extreme, can cause your world to begin falling apart. Because the emotions are so deeply hidden, the root of the problem is seldom obvious.

How Does a Child Deal with Death?

It is difficult enough for an adult to understand death, but for a child, the loss of a loved one—whether through death or separation—can be very confusing, as they have the same emotional-logical traits as the adult. The unfamiliar emotions they experience can be frightening, as they often do not know whether to cry or not to cry, to talk about it or not to talk about it. The behavior of the adults around them may add to their confusion, causing them to withdraw to a safe world without emotion, or to act out negatively for reassurance that the world will get back to normal, with the same boundaries. Just as you need to understand death and grief, so too does the child. It is important to allow the child to have some type of closure with the loved one. If your child has suffered the loss of a loved one and you notice a change in his or her behavior, I highly recommend professional counseling to avoid future problems.

There is such an intense feeling of abandonment whenever we lose a parent, but when we lose a parent to Alzheimer's, our grief is extended out over many years. That was the case for Cindy. Here is her experience with Alzheimer's.

Grieving the Loss of a Parent before His or Her Death

When my mom died, I felt a sense of peace, for I knew she was in a better place and it was her time to go. I miss her, but I know she is just a spirit away. I can still feel her presence, and sometimes I can smell her sweet breath early in the morning before consciousness.

I grieved the loss of my mom for about seven years before she died. When Mother first got sick, she had a brain aneurysm. I began grieving the loss of the mother I once had. She had brain surgery, and as a result, a bit of her personality changed, possibly the onset of Alzheimer's. There were days when she would get very moody and angry and accuse us of trying to hurt her. There were also days when she didn't recognize her family. I remember going into the room to check on her to see if she wanted coffee, and she would be so pleasant and loving. I'd think, thank you, Jesus, for bringing my mother back. But ten minutes later when I brought the coffee to her, she would be sitting on the bed crying because she was frightened, she didn't recognize her surroundings, and she didn't know who I was.

My mother was an amazing woman. She was the true matriarch of the family. She was a minister, and she walked the walk and talked the talk. Her strength and life was God. That is all she knew. That's all we knew. So when she got sick and I would see this frail, frightened woman, who was slowly losing herself and her mind, I was very angry with God for the way my mom got sick. How could God do this to someone who had dedicated her life to him? After a while I became devoid of emotions. I felt that all of life had been sucked out of me. Day in and day out, I simply existed. I then spent years being very angry. She was initially given a forty-eight-hour death sentence by the doctors, when she first got sick. She survived the brain aneurysm, and four years later she got cancer and was given three months to live. She ended up living another three years. I was still very angry with God, but I began to see how good God was to us. He gave us more time with Mother to say goodbye. She suffered for us. She hung on because we were not ready to let her go. By the time she died, I knew it was time for her to go. She said she was ready and asked me to please tell my sisters and brothers to let her go, so she could go home. I no longer have a fear of death. I have since had many loved ones die, both young and old. I seem to have a peace and under-standing of death. I don't know why, but I know that it is okay and nothing to fear. I thank God every day for the wisdom and blessings he has bestowed upon me.

Grieving the Loss of a Child

I first met Brad when he came to me for help with a hip problem. The outcome of our first session held quite a surprise for Brad. The spirit of his three-month-old baby, who had recently died, came through to me at the beginning of our session. Only a parent's words can fully express their experience, so I will let a letter from Mary (Brad's wife) speak for itself.

"There is an increased risk that your baby has Down syndrome." These are the words that many expecting parents fear the most. When my husband, Brad, and I heard them, we were devastated. What does it mean to have Down syndrome? we wondered. We had just com-pleted a nuchal translucency test, where the doctor measures the fold of skin on the baby's neck through sonogram. We only wanted to do the test in order to receive some peace of mind about our baby's health, because I was thirty-eight years old. The test had the opposite effect on us, so we had further testing done. We already had decided that no matter what we found, we would welcome the baby into our lives. After an amniocentesis test, we were told that Josh for sure had Down syndrome. I remember how I felt when we got the call that the test was positive. I felt like someone in my family had died. Having lost both my parents already, I knew the feeling well. Thinking back, I guess I felt the loss of the baby that we thought we were having. Brad and I cried in each other's arms. As upset as I was, I remember telling him, "I just *know* that everything is going to be okay." God was giving me comfort. After a few weeks, we became more and more used to the idea of our baby having Down syndrome. Eventually, we were resolved to that fact and accepted what was to be. We would say that we were not perfect, so how could we expect our baby to be? We believed that Josh's little soul chose us, and we were simply going to love him.

My pregnancy with Josh was very stressful. Just after we would become accustomed to one bit of news, the doctor would discover another problem. After we discovered he had Downs, we found out that he also had a heart problem. A couple of months later they found that Josh had an intestine problem that caused him to be unable to drink amniotic fluid. He could not keep it down. My stomach was enormous because I was so backed up with fluid. I grew to be the size of full-term twins, even though I had only one baby inside of me. We were told these two problems were 100 percent operable.

When it came time to give birth, we decided jointly with our doctor to take Josh by cesarean section. I had already been in labor for twenty-four hours, and Josh was showing no signs of emerging. Since I had to be put under general anesthesia for the C-section (there were complications getting my stomach numb), I awakened the day after his birth and had not even laid eyes on him. Brad saw him the night he arrived and said he was beautiful and how much he loved him. I was so exhausted from surgery that I remember being afraid of how I would feel about him. Fear of the unknown coupled with morphine can cloud a person's thinking. That morning a new nurse came in to take care of me and asked how my baby was. When I told her that I had not yet seen him, she could not believe this. "I have worked here for twenty years," she stated, "and sometimes you just have to break the rules." I will never forget this woman. Her name was Merrill. She wheeled my whole bed and everything that was attached to it into the Neonatal ICU to see my baby. Brad was right—he was beautiful. He was getting a bath in preparation for his first surgery and was crying furiously at the time of our arrival. As soon as they put him on my chest, he became silent. It was a divine moment. It is as if he was thinking, "Thank God you're finally here. I didn't know if I'd hear your voice again." He seemed so comforted by my voice. It was a blessing to connect with him. I sang to him like I did all the months I carried him: "You are my sunshine, my only sunshine. You make me happy when skies are gray." I will remember that moment for as long as I live. I was a real mama. The name Joshua means "the Lord is my redeemer." He was perfectly named.

When I returned home from the hospital, it was without our baby boy. He still had two surgeries to endure before we could have our bundle of joy home. He came through the first, his intestine surgery, with flying colors. We were so happy and relieved. A week later he had his heart surgery. I was still recovering from my cesarean at home. Even though I did make it to the hospital every day for a short time, it felt like torture not being there for my child. Shortly after his surgery was complete, Brad called me at home and said that things were not going smoothly with his recovery. Josh was a different color on each side of his body. They had to rush him back for a second heart operation just hours after the first one. It seems the doctor had not widened Josh's artery enough. Brad asked the doctor if Josh's little body could endure another surgery, and he was told that he *had to*. I felt so powerless and alone at home. The only thing I could do was pray. I remember telling Brad through my tears, "I don't want to start over trying to get pregnant with another baby. I want this baby! I don't care if he has Down syndrome or anything else." After the surgery was completed, Josh's heart surgeon spent the night in a chair at his bedside. His condition was very serious.

Our baby stayed in the hospital for the rest of his short life. He moved into the Pediatric ICU (PICU), where he stayed for two and a half months. Brad and I visited him every day and gave him as much love as we could around all the tubes and wires that were attached to his small body. The love that we felt for Josh was magical. It surpassed any extra chromosome that made up his anatomy. I thought he was perfect, if only he could become physically healthy. I only got to hold my angel seventeen times. He was attached to a ventilator for most of his life, which is very sensitive to movement. If it had been pulled out of place, he could have died. In short, this was what was keeping him alive and breathing. We established very strong relationships with the doctors and nurses in the PICU. I grew to feel like they were my colleagues and friends. They all loved Joshy. We called him the Rush Chairman of the PICU (like in fraternities and sororities), because everyone knew Josh and he initiated all the new resident doctors.

Over several weeks, the staff tried four times to take our baby off the ventilator, but he just could not breathe without that tube down his throat. More testing was ordered to determine what the problem was. The staff could not understand why he could not breathe on his own. They had fully expected him to heal from all of his obstacles. The doctor said that until we had answers, we would forge ahead and Josh would tell us if or when he could not sustain this pace any longer. They biopsied his lung and found that he had a nontreatable, noncurable form of a disease called lymphangectasia. His lymphatic system was not able to drain properly, and his lungs repeatedly filled with fluid. He would never be able to breathe on his own, and his lungs would continue to fill. The news was devastating.

The night before he died, I spent the night with Josh. A nurse had exchanged his crib for a twin bed so I could lie next to him. "I cannot stand seeing you curled up in a ball in that crib anymore!" she exclaimed. I had been squeezing in next to him, since I was not allowed to hold my boy. That night, things happened that had never happened before. I put my finger in my son's little hand and he squeezed it repeatedly throughout the night. It was very special. I knew that he was telling me goodbye and that he loved me. I imagined him to be saying, "It will be okay, Mama. God will take care of you." Another thing that happened that night was that Josh's blood pressure and heart rate kept dropping. The alarms on the machines sounded all night. Josh had begun to tell us that he could not go on any longer. The next day was Friday, June 18. Josh died at about 1 p.m. Although it was the hardest experience of my life, in a way, we had been preparing for it all along. We had been hoping against hope that he would survive, but there were so many problems and ups and downs in his treatment. His status had changed drastically numerous times. When the time came, we just seemed to have all the strength we needed to let our little boy go. The strength seemed to come from nowhere. I think Josh made this excruciating time easier for us. I rocked and held him without any lines attached to him, as I had longed to for so long. He was so beautiful; I did not want to let him go. Our little boy had fought as hard as he could, and it was time for everyone to give in.

I met Linda Drake about four months after Josh's passing. I was about one month pregnant with our new baby. I had heard about her through Brad. Someone had referred him to her for help with his hip problem. When I listened to their taped conversation, I had to get over to see her myself. She actually contacted Joshua. She told us that the baby I was carrying was the return of Josh's soul. I was and am still so excited, as I am now three months pregnant with our new baby. We affectionately refer to this new baby as Porkchop, until we know what sex it is. The thought of uniting with Josh's soul again is thrilling beyond belief. I have missed my baby so much throughout the last five months. This is a gift from God. Linda also told us that in a former life, Josh was a doctor who treated children. He lost a lot of his patients and never got used to the sadness he felt. She said he wanted to come back as a terminally ill child so he could teach other doctors. He chose us as parents because he knew we would not terminate the pregnancy. My experience with Linda has been such a blessing. I truly value her talents and gifts. Getting to talk to Josh through her has absolutely been enlightening and has made my pregnancy easier. It has helped me see the perfection in even our terribly painful experience. We are so proud to have been Josh's parents, and being able to unite with his blessed soul again is an honor, a joy, and a privilege!

I can't tell you how touching it was to work with this couple. The respect and support that they show each other is truly a tribute to their love. I was so honored to communicate with the spirit of little Josh. When he explained to me the purpose of the challenges of his previous life, I was stunned. Before we come into each lifetime, we work with our support group, comprised of our angels, our spirit guides, and God. They help us understand our options, as well as the challenges of our chosen paths. As Josh explained to me, he had been very adamant about what he desired to accomplish in his life. In a previous lifetime, he had been a doctor struggling with his inability to save the lives of critically ill children because of the lack of knowledge about their illnesses. In this lifetime he chose to devote his short life to helping doctors gain a better understanding of those illnesses. Because of the many unusual medical challenges of his tiny body, doctors were gathered from all medical fields to study his case. Through this experience they were given the opportunity to gain a greater knowledge of previously mysterious illnesses, assisting them in finding answers to heal children with these same challenges in the future. He said that he had carefully chosen his parents, praying daily that they would have the strength to help him fulfill his destiny. I commented to Josh that I was amazed by his selfless sacrifice. He proudly explained to me that it was no sacrifice—it was *his* life purpose, and his short life and what it brought to others would be a positive influence on everyone who knew him or heard his story.

Mary and Brad have now become the proud parents of a healthy baby boy. You can imagine the joy they are experiencing.

chapter four

Communicating with the Other Side

Sometimes we do not take or have the opportunity to heal with those we love before they die. Through repeated experiences, I have found that the ability to communicate with those in spirit is very healing for loved ones and friends left behind.

When I began communicating with spirits from the other side, it was a total shock for me. This gift first demonstrated itself for me at a meta-physical-health expo. I had a booth in which I was doing energy work. A woman had come to me with a physical problem, and I was doing Reiki energy healing on her injured knee when a man appeared beside her and began talking to me about her. Without thinking, I simply relayed his message to her. He talked about her difficulty with their family and how their youngest son was having such a hard time with his death and what he wanted her to do with certain property. He talked freely for about ten minutes while she stared at me with tears running down her cheeks.

When I finished, she thanked me repeatedly, confirming that her husband had died in an accident six months prior and what a hard time she was having, especially with her five-year-old son. She explained that the decisions she had been left with seemed overwhelming, so the messages of support she had just received were of great consolation. She thanked me again and left.

I sat there stunned, trying to comprehend what had just happened. I looked over to the man beside me, a fellow energy worker, and asked him what had happened. He was staring at me and said, "I think you just talked to a dead man." Of course that freaked me out! Talking to dead people certainly wasn't something my guides and I had previously discussed. Up to this point, I was used to channeling all kinds of messages from people's guides and angels, but I hadn't been prepared for "talking to dead people." That was *too* weird! I could not deny the fact that the healing I had seen this woman receive from her husband's message was priceless. Later, when I had time to sit down and talk with my guides, they admitted they had sneaked that one in on me. They said I would have been too scared to do it if they had told me ahead of time. They were right!

Now it gives me great joy helping people connect with their loved ones in spirit. My "introduction" to this type of conversation and reunion provided a phenomenal healing for both the wife who had been left behind and the husband who had crossed over. Having witnessed this type of healing time and time again, I am now sure there is a sign in heaven pointing down to me and others like me, enabling loved ones in spirit who are in need of healing to find us.

When doing a communication session, I am always very careful to say a prayer of protection for all involved, allowing only those of the light to enter my space.

When I first started working with those who had passed over, my father, a "good ole country boy," not truly understanding what I did, came to support me as I worked. A close friend of mine and I were side by side in a gallery setting, communicating with spirits on the other side. After witnessing the event, my father felt compelled to caution me, warning that those spirits were complete strangers and I should be careful about whom I talked to. I acknowledged that I appreciated his concern and explained that I was very careful to talk only to those that came from the light. He wasn't sure what that meant, but he somehow felt better.

When I first began my work with Spirit, I was taught to start each day with a meditation. I continue this practice even to this day. During this time I pray for those on my prayer list and ask for clarity in the messages I will give to those whom I see throughout the day. While in meditation, I often have spirits appear to me, excited about being able to give messages to their loved ones. Some I recognize, having talked to them many times before, while new ones are still unsure of how I am able to communicate for them, so they may just stand around and watch.

Communicating with the other side is now so much a part of my work that those in spirit body often come to me ahead of their living family, just to wait.

One day, as I entered my healing room, there appeared a tall man in spirit, just standing there. I was startled at first, thinking I was alone. He just said hello, that his name was Mike. I said hello and went about my business, figuring someone would be coming that day to talk to him. Strangers in spirit form walking around my house are not uncommon. I am getting used to them. (However, it does bother my two-year-old grandson. Like most young children, he is able to see those in spirit and is afraid of strangers.) I worked my way through the day talking to many people both in and out of body. When I finished the day's appointments, I noticed that Mike was still there. So I figured, well, maybe he was just here a day early.

The phone soon rang. It was a woman who said that she had been given my name by a friend and wanted to know exactly what I did. This type of call is not unusual since my contact information gets passed around by my clients. She admitted she had never done anything like this before, so she was skeptical. After quietly listening to me explain the gifts I work with, she told me that her husband had died. I asked if his name was Mike, and she excitedly said that it was. Mike and I were both relieved that I had found his family, or rather, that they had found me. He proceeded to show me a car and a Christmas tree. I asked her if her husband had died in a car wreck close to Christmas. She exclaimed that he died suddenly in a wreck on Christmas Eve. These messages were confirmation for her that this communication was real. Since Mike had left life quite suddenly, he did not have time for closure, and he needed to let her know he was still with her. She came for an appointment, we had a wonderful talk with him, and he gave many messages for her to take home to his family.

This type of communication can bring a tremendous healing for both parties.

I was allowed to be part of another such healing when Cheryl came to me trying to contact her husband. As usual, she gave me just his name, saying it was very important that she talk to him. Jeff came right through and began talking about himself and his family. He talked to us about experiences prior to his death and explained to us what he had experienced at the time of his death, since he had been alone at the time. This brought up a lot of emotions for both of them, but Cheryl needed to know the events that led up to his death. He began describing the vehicle and the circumstances of the wreck. Jeff did this in such great detail because he understood the importance of her knowing every detail about the situation. He also talked to her about the meaning of their life together and about their children. He spoke about the Christmas presents they had bought for their children. Jeff explained the specific meaning of their daughter's unusual prayer the night before his death. Had his daughter's spirit somehow known? Jeff explained how he now saw his life plan and understood how his death was part of that plan. He was supposed to have had his daughter in the car with him that day but had forgotten to pick her up. It is in times like these that we actually see that there is a plan, and the plan was not for his daughter to die, as it was only Jeff's time to leave. All of these details meant nothing to me, but it was my job to relay them to Cheryl. These messages were important in helping her understand that he was still with her and would be there to help her raise their children. As a single mother, she needed those words to help her heal the overwhelming grief that had engulfed her world.

Here is a story of healing with the other side. It is in Mary Ann's own words and has a beautiful ending.

When my husband died in late August, there were many adjustments to be made. After being a constant caregiver to a wheelchair-bound husband for eighteen months, I was alone, facing numerous challenges. I longed to know if Bill was okay on the other side. You see, after taking care of his every need for all those months, it was still in my nature to want to continue in the same role. I found myself wanting to do things for him even though he was in the spirit world. Although he had been ill with cancer for eighteen months, his death was still quite a shock to all of us, since he had been in remission for eleven months.

Through our daughter, I had heard of Linda Drake. Even though I was a bit skeptical—maybe a little more than a bit—I made an appointment with Linda for early October.

As I entered a very comfortable room, my skepticism must have been sticking out like a sore thumb. After a brief statement concerning the process of communication, Linda undoubtedly "read me like a book," because she said we would need to do energy work first. Just as quickly as she said those words she changed her mind. She said, "There is a man here . . . It is your husband." She told me that there were four spirits present. They turned out to be family members who were there with Bill. The energy work was put on the shelf for the moment, and dialogue began. Of course my quiet tears of joy and relief flowed like a small waterfall. In the couple of weeks since making the appointment, I had prayed earnestly that I would be able to communicate with Bill. I had invited him to be there for the visit. He was there, and I was overjoyed. What a special feeling!

During the visit, I shared with Linda my newfound ability to read some of the deep reading materials that Bill had always enjoyed. Before his death I had tried to read these books but found they were a little too deep for my cluttered mind. Just after telling Linda of this ability, Bill told her he sits on the bed and watches me read each night as I sit in his spot in the bedroom with his books. He shared that he was proud of what I was doing. The books discussed a person's need to discover who they are and what they want to be. After a bit more discussion, Linda had a puzzled look on her face. She said, "I don't understand this, but he shows me a pumpkin with a light inside and says you are to be a light to other people." She wondered why there was a pumpkin.

With this message I really knew Bill was there for me that day and that he had been very close to me at home. Just the day before I had printed a devotional from my computer that used a pumpkin as an example of how people are like a Jack-o'-lanterns . . . God cleanses us of the seeds of hate and thoughtlessness and plants a light within us just like we create a Jack-o'-lantern.

Since that first visit I have continued to read, meditate, and spend time praying and making myself aware that both God and Bill can give me thoughts and messages if I am just willing to listen. There were several other very personal and intimate things mentioned during the visit that only Bill could have known. He even made Linda blush.

During a visit in December, I wanted to know even more if he was really okay. He was trying to tell Linda something in a feeling manner that was difficult to understand. She asked him to tell her in a different way. As he communicated, he shared that for him now, his life was just like breathing in LOVE with each breath. How much more comforting could that be for me?

During the second visit, I said the word Granny just to see what would happen. This is what we call Bill's mother. As Linda listened to Bill, she looked at me and said, "Have you seen his mother recently?" The answer was yes. I had spent Thanksgiving with her. Bill told Linda to tell me, "Thank you for doing that for Granny, as it will be one of her last."

It is now March. There are many points of discussion in my visits with Linda and Bill that I treasure and that affirm that Bill is very close to me each and every day.

God's Grand Picture of Life

Sometimes we forget that there is a plan for our life and a purpose for every experience.

I smile each time I think of this next woman. When we first met, I was amazed by her strength and determination. She had made the unselfish choice to become a single mother of three beautiful boys. What courage she has. Here is her story.

I thank God for the spiritual gifts he gave Linda so that she could deliver the tremendous love and emotional healing to my family following the unexpected and tragic death of a very close and loved family member. I am now wondering when all of humanity will be ready to heal their hearts, clear their minds, and open their eyes to see the grand picture God has painted for each of our lives.

It is important to recognize that God's love gave us our families for all eternity. Through Linda, I have come to learn God's "grand picture of life." That is, our families, our friends, and our acquaintances never die. In fact, when their exhausting work on this earth is done, they simply leave their physical form and move closer to God's kingdom of divine love.

Once departed, our loved ones eagerly look forward to helping each of us on this earth to transform our lives by delivering beautiful messages and signs to us daily. Their signs can readily be seen when our minds are clear and our eyes are open. For those of us who have the faith of a mustard seed and believe in God's grand picture and love, we are the lucky few. This is a condensed version of my story.

It was an extremely cold winter morning on December 1, 2000. Just as I was beginning my day, the phone rang. When my brother Marc delivered the news of Jeanette's death, I immediately became weak, and, as if anesthetized, my body felt completely numb. I dropped the phone and delivered a blank stare to the universe. I was speechless. Suddenly, I felt the deepest, darkest void in my heart. I realized that the true love of my life, my friend and sister, was now gone . . . forever. While I cried uncontrollably for hours, the beautiful memories of my sister played over and over again in my mind. Jeanette was such a sweet and gentle soul, as well as a wonderful mother of two beautiful preteen boys. She had the unusual ability to instill the importance of God's love and other religious values in every life she touched. I recall how Jeanette had such an admiration for my grandmother who prayed a daily rosary. With many of our relatives in religious orders as Catholic priests and nuns, Jeanette found her spiritual path at a very early age and also prayed the rosary daily.

Jeanette's life was not at all easy, nor was mine. We came from a "greedy" and dysfunctional family of ten in which our parents were very abusive and controlling.

Suddenly my mind came racing back to the present, and I thought about Jeanette's two boys, Ivan and Nathan. How were these ten- and eleven-year-old boys handling their mother's death? I knew I had to be there for them. Within twenty-four hours, I was driving family members, in very inclement weather, to attend my sister's funeral in Indiana. Approximately two months after my sister's death, the father of her children also passed away. Prior to his passing, he gave me, in a written affidavit, his blessing and permission to raise his children.

Over the following year, I spent my time opposing my father and other family members in an Indiana guardianship proceeding where I was seeking to raise my deceased sister's children. I wanted the court to understand that I simply loved Jeanette and genuinely desired to raise her children. Close to one year later, on January 10, 2002, the judge delivered the most memorable and priceless gift I ever received in my lifetime. With the gift of two boys to raise in my sister's memory and the honorable title of "Guardian," I felt the generosity of the heavens in my life.

Until I met Linda Drake, my emotional state was compromised and in great need of repair. Even with my sister's beautiful children back in Texas and now an important part of my life, my life was still empty. Two years later, I continued to mourn and had such great difficulty accepting my sister's death. Even though I was raising my sister's two children and my ex-husband's son from another relationship, these three boys together were not healing the deep wound in my heart as quickly as I had hoped. Then, in May 2002, I purchased season passes for Schlitterbahn (a large, spectacular water park located in New Braunfels, Texas), hoping to create new beginnings in our family that would be filled with fun, laughter, and great promise.

Unfortunately, I continued to find myself weeping tears of grief uncontrollably, anywhere and anytime. Most notably, I would often find myself pulling my vehicle off a road to sit and reflect on my sister's life and her passing. And yes, the floodgates would open in tandem. For some reason, the heavens would not allow me to take my focus off my sister and her death.

Then one day my brother's very kind girlfriend, Adrienne, explained to me the possibility of reaching out to my sister on "the other side." She explained how her father had achieved such great success in business because he understood and accessed the beautiful spiritual gifts God indeed gives to certain people, gifts that can provide great wisdom from our loved ones who have passed away.

Initially, the Catholic skeptic in me delivered an emphatic "no" to this invitation. However, after considering that biblical passage from 1 Corinthians 12:4–11, where St. Paul explains different kinds of spiritual gifts from healing to prophecy, I slowly contemplated the possibility of connecting with my sister. Then six months later, after watching on television the touching work of psychic medium John Edwards, I called my friend and said, "I am ready to learn about Gods' spiritual world."

June 2002 would soon become the significant "healing" point in my life. Little did I know at the time that my perception of this world would forever be altered. The blessings and beautiful messages I would receive that day from Linda Drake would forever transform my life. Most importantly, I would be introduced to God's grand picture of life. Increasingly thereafter, I would thirst more and more for God's love, knowledge, and direction for my life path. Among other things, I would learn that before I came onto this earth, I made agreements with God about my life path and the lessons I would undertake for my spiritual growth. And on my path, I would have the opportunity to test myself and attempt to live some of those simple virtues: forgiveness, humility, and love.

While I would confront serious dysfunctional issues in my family during the session, I would also come to understand the importance of standing in the "truth" in this lifetime and engaging "wisdom" to acknowledge and remove myself from cruel, deceptive, painful, and mean-spirited situations created by the "lonely and lost" individuals around me. These individuals are lonely and lost because they have yet to see God's grand picture for their own lives.

Rather than carry negative and dark energy, which stymies spiritual growth and blocks one's own success, I came to understand the importance of releasing jealousy, bitterness, anger, and hatred from my heart. The core of my heart was to be filled with love, and I learned to forgive. Moving forward with my life required that I exercise humility and impart love along the way; impart a love that simply extends to everyone the hope for a life filled with God's love and blessings.

Within minutes of being introduced to Linda Drake's session of "spiritual healing," I was in tears. With our session being tape-recorded for all posterity, I was inspired with majestic awe as I listened to the heavens pour magical healing in my life through the kind and gentle words Linda shared with me that day. Who was giving Linda these messages about my life that were so accurate?

While I did not make the acquaintance of Linda until June 2002, it was obvious that she was providing information about my life from a most beautiful place—a place filled with such love for all humanity, a love that wanted to heal hearts and transform lives in a meaningful way. My body was overcome with great peace as I listened to Linda's angelic voice, which delivered beautiful symphonic sounds and revelations.

"You have a man standing right behind you," Linda began. "This man talks about a lot of love flowing between you, a strong connection going back two lifetimes. He did walk with you in this lifetime. He shows a big foot and a little foot, and this is a grandfather. He shows me a heart . . . This must be a grandfather. Maybe a C or a G." My stepgrandfather was Dr. George Warner, and we affectionately called him Grandpa Doc. From the onset, I felt God healing my soul.

Linda transitioned her thoughts to my life path. "They said that in this lifetime you did not choose the easy path. You chose the fulfilling path, the path that will be filled with prosperity. And again, prosperity comes in many different ways. But they say that blessings will come into your life for what you chose. Did you and your husband just divorce or something, because they are talking about a custody battle . . . Something about "fighting for children" . . . showing new beginnings and good energy around it . . . This is what was supposed to be. They said it was agreed upon before you came into this lifetime that you would raise these children . . . So you agreed with your sister and you agreed with the spirits of these children that you would be the mother. And again, they say the agreement was for "three" of them. So that was agreed. Also, they say the children would not come through you because they would be provided for you. It was an agreement that you would be the mother for these children. So with the court stuff . . . It will all fall in your favor . . ." Once again, Linda shared very accurate information. After close to a year of litigation, on January 10, 2002, I was indeed granted guardianship of my sister's children.

I also was pleasantly surprised as Linda encouraged me to take my emotions to a theme park to release frustration and enjoy life. Coincidentally, Linda did not suggest Fiesta Texas or SeaWorld, which are both close to my home. Instead, she advised me to spend time at the very theme park where I had just purchased season passes for my nephews and which was fifty miles from my home.

"Because of all of the responsibility put on your shoulders, you have forgotten how to play. You have forgotten how to interact with your inner child and do fun things because you carry such responsibility. Your inner child is saying it is time to play. We need to spend some time without responsibility . . . just having some fun. Whether or not you go to Schlitterbahn . . . do something with the kids . . . You have to have fun. Don't just turn them loose. You have to go with them and have fun . . . enjoy yourself . . . squeal and laugh and play."

Of course, in my grief, I was desperate not only to find my own healing, but also to embrace the opportunity to deliver a spiritual healing to my sister's children, who continued to experience such pangs of sadness following their mother's untimely death. After receiving such beautiful messages from Linda, I knew the spiritual magic would continue to flow and touch the gentle spirits of Nathan and Ivan, as it had mine. It was my hope that my nephews' visit with Linda would connect their souls directly to their mother's love. In all of its beauty, I would once again witness God's love, the love that allows families to stay connected until the end of time.

My nephews sat next to me during my first visit with Linda in June 2002. In their youthful innocence, they were so amazed at the accurate information a stranger was delivering to us about our lives. It was like a magic show for them. When they sat for their own tape-recorded reading that same month, their amazement turned to great happiness as they received messages from their mother and connected once again to her love.

When Jeanette's boys moved to Texas following the guardianship, we had lengthy discussions about their mother. Primarily, we discussed our beautiful memories of Jeanette. While Jeanette's boys indicated that their most treasured desire was that their mother now be with them at night to protect them as they slept, both boys also inquired about the extent of their mother's love and if she had really in fact loved them. And without any prior knowledge of their sentiments, Linda came through with answers for them from their mother that delivered such a monumental healing in their lives. Over time, their lives became noticeably happier, and the wisdom they gained about this process also helped them become more academically focused. "I see her holding a little baby about a year old . . . singing to her children. This represents her love for her children. She talks about being around you very often. She watches over her children at "night." This one can be mischievous . . . She laughs. Even when you were learning to walk, you wouldn't let anyone touch you . . . You had to do it on your own. She sends a lot of love . . . She watches over you very carefully. She has tears coming down . . . She was sorry she had to leave . . . She needs you to know that she is with you . . . She said she knew when she had to leave that you would be taken care of, and she has worked with spirit to create the energy for you to be where you are. Again, she says this was by agreement."

Toward the end of her reading with Nathan and Ivan, Linda shared my sister's message about past lifetimes. "She says she had a previous lifetime with you. These children were mine before . . . and before, I lost them. So this was her second time having to leave them behind. I see a lifetime with a covered wagon . . . the old West. And children are walking beside the wagon as they are crossing a big expanse of land. She is just talking about the children getting sick and dying. She says she knew in this lifetime that they were not hers to hold, and she was always fearful that she would lose them because she knew the time was coming."

The second visit to Linda in November 2002 was ever so memorable for Ivan. Among other beautiful messages, Linda asked Ivan, "She is talking about a birthday . . . When was your birthday? What did you do for your birthday? She said she was around him on his birthday. She said she was there. She said there were a lot of memories around the celebration of your birthday. She cries because she wants to be close to you all. She wants you to know how close she is to you . . . but she says she watches everything in your life that happens. She says she is there for you and you can talk to her anytime . . . Just call her and she is right there." For Ivan, this was the most magical birthday gift he could have ever dreamed of. He had just celebrated his birthday at a restaurant down the street from the college where his mother had taught. Ivan's godmother shared with us that she often ate at this restaurant with Jeanette.

We have had many visits with Linda since 2002. While many of my friends have gone to visit Linda for their own spiritual healing, not one has reported back to me being less than awestruck after listening to Linda's beautiful messages from "the other side" that deliver such healing. Soon I will deliver my own book to this world. I have so many more beautiful stories to share about the powerful messages from my sister provided to me by Linda, messages that guided me through very important events in my life. After close to two years of working with Linda, I am now living testimony that Linda's healing work can transform lives in such a beautiful way when one chooses to walk a more spiritual path.

Perhaps one of the more profound messages our family received from Linda is that "everybody has angels and guides around them . . . They are always there. It is just when we acknowledge and allow them to be a part of our life that they really work strongly in our life." We are so thankful for all of the healing messages that were so kindly and generously delivered to our family from my Grandpa Doc and especially Jeanette . . . a beautiful sister, loving mother, and loyal friend for all eternity.

I will share with you an experience I had while writing this book. I had just finished putting in a full day of healing sessions when I sat down to relax in front of the TV. My grandfather who had been deceased for over twenty years came to my mind. As I closed my eyes, I could see his face, with his bright blue eyes, dimples, and warm smile. As I sat reminiscing about my memories of him, the front door opened wide and then closed. My husband, who was sitting across the room, observed this, then looked over at me and calmly asked if it was someone we knew. I smiled and told him yes, it was my Grandpa Smith just giving us confirmation that he was here with us.

Do our loved ones in spirit need to open doors to come into the room? No, that was just a sign to get our attention so he could say hello. I sat for another thirty minutes or so remembering all of the wonderful memories of my childhood and feeling his love. I stilled myself long enough to listen to the thoughts and words he was giving me. He gave words of love and support as he expressed great pride in what I was doing with my life. That meant a lot to me.

When we open our minds and hearts to receive messages from our loved ones, our awareness of their presence becomes keener. Our blindness to their presence is created by our fearful perception of death. When that perception is changed or expanded, we become much more aware of the many signs that they are giving us as proof that their spirits continue to exist within our world. If we refuse to believe in their existence, it is frustrating for them, as it is extremely difficult for them to energetically manifest signs in an effort to change our minds; although if they feel this contact is necessary, they will continue to try. When we look for the signs from our loved ones, we will see them.

You Do What? Skeptics . . .

Don't mistakenly think that all of the people that come to me just walk into my office trusting that I have this gift of talking to their loved ones who have died. The concept of communication with spirits on the other side is understandably an idea that some of you may be uncomfortable with, but I hope you will approach it with an open mind. You may have seen psychics such as John Edwards, James Van Praage, or George Anderson, to name just a few, on television. Their programs about communicating with the other side are becoming quite popular, and their work is very similar to mine. There are many people with this wonderful gift, but you will not hear about most of them. I can understand their reluctance to openly reveal their gifts, as it tends to generate a flurry of judgment and criticism, as do other intuitive gifts. Most people haven't been introduced to or don't understand the spiritual concept of the intuitive world. We all have God-given gifts; how we choose to develop them or use them is our choice.

For most of the people who come to me, it is their first time to have the opportunity of communicating with their loved ones in spirit. I am quite accustomed to skeptics, so their doubts do not deter me from giving them the messages that I receive.

I will share with you this client's skepticism.

Well . . . I had this friend who went to see this psychic and, from my perspective, was having some *strange* experiences. Now, I am this logical, commonsensical, hard-core skeptic that always has to put my hand in the fire even when someone warns me it's hot! So, I decided that I had better protect my friend's best interests and made an appointment for myself to see what was going on. I don't know just what I expected to find, but nothing short of a gypsy with a crystal ball would have surprised me. Instead, I found myself sitting in front of a rather normal, pleasant, sensible woman with whom I felt instantly comfortable. *But*, I was still guarded and very careful about saying very little about myself. I decided that the best tactic was to get her to do the talking. What transpired is still one of the most memorable moments in my life.

You see, I was raised by my Aunt Pearl. She was my mother figure, best friend, mentor, inspiration, and role model, and she loved me unconditionally. She died in 1994 at the age of ninety-four. I held her in my arms at the moment of her passing. The loss has always been with me and always will. Linda, in a very matter-of-fact way, began telling me that a woman had come forward to her, and Linda physically described her. So far, so good, but she could have gotten lucky on the physical stuff. I waited to see what else she could "dream up." The first thing she said was that this woman was showing her some pictures in frames. They were black-and-white silhouettes of some kind. There was no question that this was my dear Aunt Pearl. You see, from the time I was a little girl, we always went to the county fair together. She always went to this man who made silhouette pictures using black paper and scissors. She framed these pictures of me and had them hanging in the stairway for years. I still have them. No one but me would have known about these pictures. If there was anyone who would have known about them, they would be in Illinois, not in Texas where I now live. The pictures have never been unpacked.

Other similar visions came to her that placed me in a numb state. For example, there is this oil painting. One summer when I was "bored," my aunt enrolled us in an oil painting class. She painted some work horses with a farmer undoing their harness at the end of a day of hard work. The teacher kept making her repaint the horses because they didn't look "tired" enough for work horses. She must have painted them five times. Everyone in the class kept laughing about her doing these horses. The final product hung for years in the hall. She would often go by and pat the horses on the rump and say, "I feel as tired as the poor old horses." I have the picture now and do the same some days. The reins are on the ground, as the farmer is undoing the harness. Linda kept getting the message that I was to let the reins go to the ground. I was to let loose of the reins. I believe that Aunt Pearl was trying to tell me to let go of my need to control. I was to allow myself the freedom to experience, loosen my mental grip, and grow in my trust and faith.

I just could not believe what she was telling me, and to this day I often run it through my mind like a favorite video. If it had not been my dear aunt who came forward, I would probably still be a doubting

Thomas. I left Linda with the greatest of gifts. An hour with my Aunt Pearl had given me some meaningful advice for my life once again and the knowledge that she is on the other side. Life after death does exist in some form, because she is there proving it to me. Am I still a skeptic? Yes. Does my logic get in my spiritual way? Yes. As much as before I met Linda? No. I believe differently now, and my metaphysical connection has grown in giant steps. Welcome to another dimension, dear skeptical friends!

This next story was written by Jon's wife, as she knew this session would challenge him but she felt he needed the healing it would bring.

I brought my skeptical husband, Jon, to a session with Linda. Having no prior experience with psychics or healing, he questioned her intensely about the difference between angels and guides, and how she did what she did.

Linda explained that he actually had a spirit with him that had chosen to be "like" a guide for him. This spirit was with him at that very moment. She described the spirit as a person who had previously been a loving, nurturing father figure to him as a child. The spirit had been available for emotional and moral support during difficult periods when his father had abandoned the family and his mother was working many hours a week to support the family.

Surprised, Jon said, "That sounds like my Uncle Bo."

Linda started writing in the palm of her hand with her finger. She was being given letters, and was trying to put them together. She spelled out A-M-D-R-O-N. She said AMDRON three times, while Jon was looking very puzzled. He admitted that the name AMDRON meant nothing to him.

Linda just passed it by and continued to tell Jon that this person had chosen to be like one of his spirit guides to help him with his chosen path. This spirit was the one that helped him figure things out when he felt stuck.

All of a sudden, Jon had a revelation. He stopped the session, reached over to Linda's table, and retrieved one of her business cards. Picking up a pen, he wrote something on the back side and then gave it to her.

He had made an anagram of AMDRON and turned it into RAMOND.

He quietly told Linda that his Uncle Bo's real name was Ramond.

As this session demonstrated, I am sometimes given bits of information, like clues. They are not for me to figure out; I am just the messenger. The information is for you, as confirmation that further information given to you is real. Many times I just sit and relay information, whether it is about a person, a court case, or a particular situation. This information often makes no sense to me at all, so I just relay it as I hear it. Sometimes it won't make sense to you at the time either, but I always ask that you hold on to it, because it will eventually. I frequently have clients call me months later saying, "Remember when you told me this and this? Well, it turned out to be very important information that I needed to hear. Thank you." I have learned to trust Spirit and stay out of my own judgment.

Many people come to me as skeptics and leave as believers. You may not get all of the answers you want, but your loved ones in spirit will share with you a word or piece of information that no one else could know. They are trying to give you confirmation that they are still with you, giving you guidance and knowledge that there is life after death. When I receive information from those in spirit, they give me messages in many ways. Sometimes I see an image of them, or hear words, or they show me pictures, or I may smell a fragrance. They will use all of our senses as tools to communicate with us.

chapter five

Healing with Our
Loved Ones in Spirit

In this book I will share with you many stories of healing with the other side. Sometimes it is our inner child that needs to heal with a loved one who has crossed over. As difficult as this sounds, with Spirit anything is possible. It can be an extremely powerful and life-changing event.

Sometimes it is surprising what mental or emotional blockages we hold from our childhood experiences. Rita was generous enough to share with us her healing session in which the spirit of her deceased father assisted us.

The Gift Beyond Monetary Value

My father enjoyed good health throughout much of his life. It was a surprise to us when, at the age of eighty-seven, he was diagnosed with lung cancer. The doctor estimated he had six months to live. As best we could, Dad and I said our goodbyes and frequent "I love you's" to make up for all those not voiced in the years past. The doctor was painfully accurate, and Dad died in April 2000.

Two years later, I had a sense of unsettled business with my father and saw Linda to heal the karma between our souls. As Linda started the session, Dad was eager to begin and often interrupted Linda, trying to hurry us along. This was one of Dad's signature trademarks throughout my life. "He's already here. He's working to help you," she said. Linda asked him to be patient, as she explained what we would be doing.

"The alcohol killed your father?" Linda asked, referring to his drinking.

"No, the diagnosis was lung cancer," I said.

"He says the alcohol took his life away. The alcohol took everything from him," she paused, patiently waiting for more to be revealed to her. "It took away his participation in life," she said. Yes, my father had been an alcoholic.

I was moved. Years earlier, when I told my parents I was an alcoholic, I didn't feel they understood what that meant. Like most alcoholics, I can remember the first time I got drunk. I was thirteen and I liked the way alcohol made me feel. There was a false sense of euphoria, of the pieces of my life locking into place, a sense of feeling complete. I was drinking a margarita and quickly drank another and another, trying to extend this magical feeling. Before long, I'd had too much and got sick. That didn't deter me. I wanted that feeling again, and I began drinking in pursuit of that exhilaration. One day, when I was eighteen, I wrote in my diary, "I think I have a problem with alcohol." It had been barely five years since my first drunk, but I couldn't stop on my own and I kept drinking. At twenty-eight, I was led to Alcoholics Anonymous and got sober. I learned to use the twelve steps of recovery to change, from the inside out. While recovery was a life-changing experience for me, I learned I couldn't recruit friends and family into this way of life. Unless someone is ready, they don't want it. My family accepted that I didn't drink, but we never talked about why or how.

When my father died, I'd been sober for seven years, and I carried an AA chip, marking my length of sobriety. Before closing my father's casket, I gave him my chip. Choking back tears from the memory, I told Linda, "It was my intent to give to him that which I value most."

"He acknowledges that," Linda said, as she channeled his spirit. "'The gift beyond monetary value,' that's the way he puts it," Linda said. "He says it should have been the other way around—him teaching you, not you teaching him. He said he was never strong enough and didn't value the right things or the right people in life," Linda told me. "He said he valued his friends more than his family because with his family, he felt guilt . . . He said he wasted so much of his life. He's ready to heal."

My inner child told Linda about the loss and confusion she felt growing up. "She felt responsible for her father's drinking. She thought if she made him happy at home, he wouldn't drink. She said she couldn't make him love her enough . . ." Linda said, "He says, 'You were left in the shadows.'" We talked for a while when Dad interrupted again. "He keeps saying, 'Let's go, let's go.'"

Linda described how we would be digging deep down into my subconscious, into my childhood, to let my little girl voice her anger.

"Let her start to be truthful," Linda said. "When we go in to do the healing, we go in for the strong emotions that are still affecting your life. We're going to rile up all the emotion. It's not just healing the surface stuff. It's getting down deep to what the cause was and who created it for you."

My dad was fifty-two when I was born, and I was his youngest daughter. We did not have a close relationship. This was partly due to my fierce self-determination.

Linda shared his comments. "As a toddler, you wanted to walk by yourself without any help . . . 'The one of independence,' he called you. Throughout your life your words were, 'No, I can do it myself.'"

The barrier in our relationship was partly due to my father's limitations in showing love or affection. As Linda explained, my loss was small compared to what he felt as a child. He had feelings of being abandoned, feelings of being afraid. I knew my father lost his father at an early age and was taken from his mother. Raised by an uncle, he often went hungry, and money was scarce.

"He knew nothing about touching and feeling, emotional and nurturing love," Linda explained. "He did the best he could. He did not understand what your needs were or what his needs were. He said he always felt very alone. He didn't want you to feel alone, but he didn't know how to touch your heart. There was always the barrier between you.

"As a child, he knew that money could buy a lot of things he never had. He felt money could replace for you what he never had. He said his childhood was pinching pennies, full of a lot of fear. He said he never wanted you to have financial fear."

In hindsight, my father provided food, shelter, and an education—three essential things lacking in his own childhood. But what I craved was his love and attention.

"It's a great gift to release any anger, pain, fear, any negative emotion or belief, that was created in you. It is a gift to give this back to your father, because when he created those emotions he created an energy, a karma," Linda said, as we began the healing.

She asked me to be specific with my thoughts and emotions so that I could acknowledge and release any remaining pain or negative belief systems that might be deep within my subconscious. She explained that God would allow my father to see and understand what was created and why I felt anger and pain. God would heal my father of this karma so he could go on his path without carrying the burden of what was created with me. "We're going to release all the belief systems that your little girl (inner child) took on that belonged to her father. God goes within you and heals your heart. Sounds really weird and involved, but as long as God's doing it, it works," she said.

Linda used Reiki energy to align my chakras and to bring in God's healing energy. She instructed me to repeat after her, "I acknowledge and choose to release all negative energies created between my father and myself from this lifetime and past lifetimes."

We began untangling my pain as we released to my father the negative emotions and beliefs that had been created in me:

I release my father's judgment of me, that I could not please him.

I release my anger about your drinking. I thought I'd done something wrong.

I release my pain when you would leave because of your anger. I was scared you weren't coming back.

I release you for not showing me how to be angry at someone but still love the person.

I release my anger that you could be loving and generous with strangers but not with me.

I release you for not being the father that I wanted.

I release you for teaching me that alcohol is a way to hide emotions.

I release the belief that you created my alcoholism.

I release my anger because you feared being yourself.

I release all guilt that I could not help you.

I release the belief that you did not value me for who I was and for who I am.

I release the belief that you weren't enough, that I wasn't enough.

I release all that comes between us.

I release the need to have your approval to be successful.

I release your belief system about love and money being equal.

Linda asked me to describe what money meant to me. "It can come and go. It's mysterious. I don't know why I'm compelled to get rid of it," I said.

"That's a lot like your father," Linda pointed out. "Did you feel like your father wanted you? Did you deserve your father? Did you deserve money?" I replied no to each of her questions.

She asked me to repeat the following:

I release the belief system about what money is.
I release the belief that I am not worthy of money.
I release the need to push it away from me.
I release my connection between money and my father.

Linda had me replace my old belief system with affirmations:

Money is earned by hard work.
I am worthy of money.
I release all fear of money and of it abandoning me.
Money is good.
I want money.
I can be successful.
I am successful.
I am powerful.

She asked me to describe love. "Love is earned. As a child, love was not abundant in my home. I wanted more love," I said.

"Did you feel starved of love? Unworthy of love? You felt afraid of love because it would be taken from you. Isn't that what you thought about money?" she asked. Again, I repeated after her:

I accept love.
I am worthy of unconditional love.
I release the belief that love has to be earned.
I trust love.
I release all fear of love, of being abandoned by love.
I release all pain I have felt from love.
I accept love and my worthiness to have love.
I accept money and my worthiness to have money.
I can be successful without fear of it abandoning me, as I am worthy
*   of it.*
I am free of the fear of rejection.
I release all shame of being rejected by others.

Linda prayed, "I ask God, in your strength and wisdom . . . that all of the energies that were placed in this basket are released from

Rita. I ask that all cords be cut, as they are no longer hers to hold. I ask that your father receive it with open arms and open heart." Linda paused. "He asks for your forgiveness." I gave Dad my forgiveness, and we continued.

"I ask God to stand him in his white light of unconditional love," Linda continued. "I ask God to place his arms around him and place him in a gold, iridescent bubble of healing. I release you to God and ask him to heal you of not just this karma but all the other karma you created in this lifetime."

She instructed me to honor my little girl (inner child), to take her to do something she enjoys, and to allow her to be part of my daily life. "God's going to put a beautiful pink light into your heart, filling you with unconditional love and healing. You've freed her of the burden that's held her back her whole life of feeling she was not loved by him, of not getting what she needed from him. We released your father's belief system that was instilled in you about your worthiness for love and money. It was his, in the beginning. He gave it to you to carry. Now you've given it back to him. It's no longer yours. You have to reexamine what money means and allow yourself to receive it. Receive your success. Now, you have a wide-open path, and you can go as fast as you want down that path. There's no blockage there for you anymore. It's up to you what you want to create in your life. Change how you perceive it."

Linda told me to proclaim to the universe:

I am worthy of prosperity.
I am worthy of the right job, at the right time, for the right amount of money.

"When it comes, don't say, 'I don't have the tools for this.' Step out and believe in yourself and take off. The tools will be given to you. Spirit wouldn't bring you the job if Spirit didn't think you could do it. But you have to go out there and look for it. They have to know you're motivated enough that you want that job and feel like you deserve it. Change the way you feel about yourself. They have changed the perspective of who the little girl is and what she is worthy of."

The whole time Linda was talking, she was working, releasing blocked energy and creating a pathway for new energy.

Finally, my homework assignment was to draw a picture of myself and surround it with affirmations of what I am: beautiful, powerful, loveable, smart. "You are re-creating who you are. You get to be who you want to be. Draw that picture and believe in the person you have created. You have all the abilities, the education, everything to do what you want to do."

These resentments and memories were all the things that had been left unsaid over a lifetime. My father didn't know about them, and now, for the first time, I was telling him. I was no longer blaming him or holding on to these resentments. My father and I were beginning to heal. Finally, I was releasing both of us from my pain.

Today, I'm a chemical dependency counselor, in the first year of my internship. I help women learn to live clean and sober and find the gift beyond monetary value.

Another story of healing after death is shared by Kenneth. I met Kenneth and his family at a psychic fair. We have since had numerous sessions together, covering everything from healing the inner child to past-life regression work. This is Kenneth's description of our work together, and I thank him for his generosity in sharing with us the personal emotions of his experiences. I know it will touch the hearts of many of you and give you a better understanding of how you can heal even the deepest pain.

Linda, I feel as if I must start by telling you a little of my background so that you may better appreciate the effect you have had on my life.

As I look back, my spiritual path has been a strange one. For the first ten years of my life, I never entered a church door. For the next ten years, I entered our church every time the door was open, which was three times a week plus revival meetings, church camps, etc. My family and most of our small rural community experienced a very real spiritual awakening via a loving and charismatic preacher. While he was alive, his example and leadership kept us all together in a loving, spiritual embrace. When he died and was replaced by a rule-mongering fundamentalist type of preacher, everything quickly disintegrated for me. As I was just entering adolescence, this couldn't have happened at a worse time. Fundamentalist Christian dogma can be a very harmful and devastating thing when taken too seriously, and oh, how seriously did I take it! Imagine being a teenage boy and thinking that if you look upon a woman with lust you have truly committed the equivalent of adultery. And then knowing (not just believing) that if I were then to die in a car accident, I would go to a very real fiery hell for eternity—just for looking. I was haunted and consumed with trying to follow all of the rules, and looking back, I realize I could only have been described as clinically depressed.

Things changed for me overnight. In the midst of soul searching over my plight, I experienced a true epiphany. I gained a new concept of God: He is the brain of the universe that is literally alive. Words cannot describe what a gift my new God was. The freedom to think and wonder without guilt was liberating and empowering. Releasing Fundamentalist Christianity truly made me feel "born again." I changed my college major from business to sociology and psychology. I read the words of Jesus in a new light, realizing for the first time that he taught against the "mindless rule of following" that had plagued my adolescence. His Golden Rule corresponded nicely to the unconditional love I was studying in the social sciences.

Over the next three decades, through marriage, career, children, and many ups and downs, I was a more content and mainstream person, but gradually became less spiritual. I didn't believe in hell but also doubted that there was a heaven. The resurrection of Jesus, angels, etc., seemed unlikely, and I'd never heard of spirit guides until about three years ago, when my daughter, Adrienne, started talking about them along with other seemingly outrageous New Age ideas. Fearing for her mental health, I decided to read some of what she was reading, largely just to be able to argue with her. To my surprise, Michael Newton's book *Journey of the Soul* rang true, and I decided to have an open mind on the subject.

I went to my first psychic fair about two years ago along with my family. I told my daughter that I wanted to talk to a psychic and asked whom I should see. She suggested you, Linda. That short fifteen minutes, as I immediately told Adrienne while in a daze, was one of the most profound experiences of my life. The first thing you said was that my mother was there. I ignored this, determined not to fall into a false psychic trap. I asked if you could see my spirit guide. You immediately gave the exact description that someone else had given me, but you couldn't make out his name at first. Then suddenly, you said his name was Raven of the Moon (Ra-Mu was the name I had been given before). You said we'd had a past life together and that he'd been my main spirit guide in this lifetime.

I was spellbound. Instantaneously I had become a believer in the other side. The readings given to the rest of my family were also profound, and all of them taken together were truly amazing. It wasn't just the individual information given that was convincing, but the manner in which it was given. There was no hocus-pocus. You were just sitting there doing your job, suffering terribly with hay fever but still just plugging along. And after talking to each other afterward and listening to each other's tapes, it was very evident that you really were receiving from somewhere and then transmitting to us. You weren't making up anything. It was more as if you were a foreign language translator. You looked and listened and then told us what you perceived, and this had included communication with my own deceased mother!

In subsequent readings with you, my mother always appeared with messages concerning my childhood that, frankly, I thought to be irrelevant. It was amazing to be hearing from her, but I thought we had settled all of our personal problems from my childhood. You said I had not and needed to experience inner-child healing. I was familiar with the therapeutic technique of finding your inner child as a means of healing old wounds, and I know that ordinarily with traditional therapists this would take months, if not years. You said it could be done in one or two sessions. I said, "Why not try it?" You had me keep a picture of myself as a child around and tune into him from time to time until the appointment. You started the session much like a traditional therapist by having me describe my childhood. The big difference, though, was that my deceased mother was there, agreeing or disagreeing with what I said. I remember asking her at one time if just because she was now on the other side, did this make her omniscient (knowing everything)? You (and she) said that today's session would primarily be a healing with my father, who is still living. From my viewpoint I had a good relationship with him, so this statement came as a surprise.

The next part of the session began by my lying on a massage table. You did some energy work, and you invoked the help of God, spirit guides, and whatever to aid in the healing process. You then helped me walk back in time, and I started not just talking about, but feeling, what I experienced in my childhood. You talked me through, as you had me picture putting these feelings in one or as many sacks as it took and then destroying them. From about age three until age ten, these feelings involved just my mother, and many sacks had to be used as we went through the experiences. Then at age ten, just after we'd started going to church, came the most traumatic occurrence of my childhood. For the sake of brevity, let's just say it involved sex, and the situation couldn't have been handled any worse by my parents. Their reaction, along with my religious experiences, is what sent me into depression. But reliving this particular experience with you, Linda, made me suddenly realize that most of my anger was at my father. He had completely stayed out of the situation and left my mother to handle everything.

At this point in our session, I remember exclaiming, "I'm being raised by idiots!" My anger at my father was voluminous. At a time when I most needed an understanding male figure, he had completely struck out and left me at the mercy of my mother, who was very incompetent at handling the situation. Years later, after my spiritual epiphany and social science studies, I had come to peace with my mother and hadn't realized that my father was even involved. Now my anger was boiling, and it would take much more than a sack to contain it. I pictured a huge hot air balloon being filled with my anger, then still another, before I was emptied. So this was why my deceased mother had been so insistent! She was getting all of the blame and knew I needed to see the part my father had played in this by his absence.

Other occurrences with him came up as our session continued, and we ended with a "cord cutting." (The next day Dad told me he had become inexplicably depressed for about an hour the day before, and I feel sure it was during this time.) As for me, the next day I began to cry when describing the cord cutting to my wife, Jan. But my relationship with my father has improved ever since. Physically, for several days after the cord cutting, I experienced a burning in my throat and stomach area even while taking Nexium and Tums. I knew I really had experienced a phenomenal healing. From what I know of traditional psychotherapy through my own studies and training (I have received counselor training on the master's level), as well as having listened to my psychiatrist brother for many years, what had happened to me in that one session was impossible. Any rational person knows these things take years to heal! But now I know they are wrong!

Kenneth's father passed away about a year after we did his healing work. In our most recent session, we discussed how he was doing with his grief. Kenneth shared with me how he felt that he was doing surprisingly well and attributed that to all of the work we had done with his inner-child issues. During the last year of his father's life, their relationship had become better than ever. Their final days together were not filled with anger, judgment, or regrets, as is the case for many of us. They were able to have the father-son relationship, full of love and acceptance, that Kenneth had always desired, and that was the greatest gift he could have received from and given his father.

The emotional trauma that we experience after the loss of a loved one can be devastating, but the knowledge that they are still with us can bring us so much comfort. Knowing that they are there with us as we grieve, giving their love and support through our healing process, is a tremendous relief. The support of their presence can enable us to move forward with our lives. You won't stop missing their physical presence or the sound of their laughter, but knowing that their spirit is still alive and well can bring you great comfort. They understand God's plan for us, and they understand that they completed their life purpose, enabling them to go home, and they want to support you while you complete yours.

Through this next story, I hope you will understand how powerful your loved ones in spirit can be. During our session, Melanie's deceased father gave her many signs and messages as confirmation that he understood the challenges she had endured. His desire to heal the karma between them assisted in freeing her from the beliefs that held her stuck in an unproductive life, believing it was what she deserved.

I was the scapegoat child in a dysfunctional family. From my earliest memories until I moved away from my hometown at the age of thirty-four, I had been the peacekeeper of the family—because if the family was at peace, no one would blame me for something. Whatever went wrong, it was my fault, even if I was ten miles away at the time. I could never do anything right, in their eyes. I was a failure, in their eyes. My mother used to laugh about my sister (who was eighteen months older than I, and my only sibling) hitting me while I was a newborn in the crib. My sister actually told me that she resented me because of my middle name! I know it's ridiculous, but she was serious and is still resentful into our adulthood. My entire family, on both sides, openly judged and ridiculed and hated me.

My father passed away in 1975, at the age of forty-nine years and nine days. I had never really known him; in fact, I felt more comfortable at home when he was not there. Truly, I have no memories of my parents being kind to each other. They were either fighting or not living together, and they divorced when I was ten years old. In-laws hated in-laws. On top of all that, my mother encouraged me to go, alone, to the movies or to the public swimming pool with her suitor (a co-worker of my father's, incidentally), then spend the night with him. This occurred on at least three occasions that I can remember. I was an innocent, naive ten-year-old child, and I was being sexually molested by my mother's boyfriend, with my mother's encouragement.

I met Linda Drake in the spring of 2002. When I sat down in the pink chair, I asked her if anyone was with us. She said, "Your father's here. He's taking full credit for bringing you to me." That was the beginning of my relationship with my dad. That first day, Daddy explained so many things that I had been too young to understand. Daddy confessed that he had never really known me (ditto), and he apologized for that. In fact, he took full responsibility for not being there when I needed him. That day, I could have talked with him for hours. There was so much I wanted to say to him and hear him say to me. That first day, going home on the freeway, I felt like I was floating on a cloud. My dad was my co-pilot, and he's been my co-pilot ever since. Many sessions later, I asked Daddy why he chose to die at so young an age. He said that his work on earth was done and that he could do more good from the other side, and now that I've gotten to know him, I believe that to be so.

Through Linda, I learned that my life themes during this incarnation were judgment and abuse. It took a while for my hard head to accept it, but eventually, through Linda's kindness and at my spirit guide's insistence, I learned that I wrote these themes into my blueprint. I learned that I actually chose my mother and father. As horrible as it was, I came to realize that judgment and abuse (mental as well as physical) were part of my life's lessons. They were the issues I had come into this life to experience. I had to understand them and heal them to move forward with my life. I followed Spirit's directions to the T, wrote the letter to my mother, and forgave her and my other family members for treating me the way they did—after all, they were just cast members following the script that I had written in my far-off-Broadway play.

Although I choose not to associate with those family members, I am at peace with myself. I have resolved the issues that tormented me for so long. I am happy and healthy, and I am adored by my husband and loved and respected by my children and grandchildren.

During the past three years, through her gifts, Linda has healed my wounds, given me support in uncertain times, and encouraged me to hang in there when I doubted my role in this incarnation. At times I proved to be a stubborn pupil, not heeding Linda's counsel. I was going through a difficult two-and-a-half-year period where I was unemployed, or employed for short stints with very mean and cruel employers (part of my lesson). Finally, in the fall of 2003, at the psychic fair, Spirit came through forcefully and gave Linda the words to tell me exactly what I needed to do to work through the blockage that was affecting my life so negatively. I remember her saying, as she tapped her microphone, "Is this thing on?? [tap tap] Cause I want you to hear this!" And boy, did I ever heed her words that time!

That was the first day of the next stage in my life. I followed her instructions to the letter, and violà! Two weeks later I was offered a very rewarding position with a law firm. My husband and I are moving forward with our lives, discarding negativity and blockages. It's almost like we have fallen in love all over again. I would never have known how to solve the issues weighing me down from my childhood without Linda's guidance and my father's messages.

If, as children, we are made to feel that we are unworthy of receiving love, attention, or respect, this is the pattern that is created in our lives. That was the pattern of abuse that Melanie had created for her life. The child felt that if her family didn't value her, how could she value herself? It wasn't until her deceased father came to her to show his love and appreciation for her, in a way that he was unable to while he was alive, that Melanie's perception of herself changed. The healing that Melanie received from her father was priceless; it changed many aspects of her life.

chapter six

Signs from Our Loved Ones in Spirit

Many times we are given signs and messages of our loved one's presence. It is our choice as to how we perceive these signs and messages, but they are real. We can continue to have a spiritual relationship with our loved ones even though they are in spirit. This brings great comfort to some people, as they move through their stages of grief. Other people prefer to close the door and grieve in their own way. It is a personal decision.

Elizabeth lost her husband to cancer after thirty-four years of marriage and raising a family together. I regret that I had known Robert and Elizabeth for only three months before Robert passed. I am grateful for the opportunity to have been with them through this experience, because I learned so much about life and death from Robert before he passed, as well as afterward. Elizabeth's spiritual progress has been amazing, and I am privileged to have been a part of that.

Here is Elizabeth's experience with the loss of her husband and her grief:

My best friend, my soul mate, my husband, Robert, died on April 22, 2000, at 9:11 a.m., after being diagnosed in early January 2000 with bone cancer. Those four and a half months of watching his body decline at an alarming rate were devastating for us both, but he was the one with severe physical pain. He delayed taking medication as long as he possibly could, so that he could be lucid enough to help me and our family make the transition. In effect, I think he taught me how to die with grace and dignity. During this period I asked him to give me a sign after he passed so I would know that his spirit was with me—a selfish request, I admit. I have always been a believer in God and his promise of eternal life; however, being human I suppose I wanted proof.

One morning several months later, I put on my watch that Robert had given me. I noticed that it had stopped at 9:11, the time of Robert's death. I immediately felt an inner knowing that this was the sign. Then doubt set in. Maybe I need a new battery, I thought. I went ahead and reset the watch to the proper time, and it's been keeping perfect time since and it's now 2004 with that same old battery.

Many other things have gotten my attention, such as dimming lamp lights and the TV going off all by itself. I know that Robert's spirit is with me, and we often talk and walk together in my dreams.

The most memorable occurrences have been when I've gone to Linda for Reiki treatments. Robert always shows up with a message for me. While I am lying there looking up at the ceiling, a rainbow always appears without a logical cause. Last month I received a treatment just a few days before my birthday. As I lay looking up at Linda's ceiling, not only did a rainbow appear but it was huge and shaped like a heart, and inside the rainbow heart was a spot of white light that morphed into a dragonfly with wings fluttering! Really fluttering—I could not make this up—it was a miracle! What a great birthday present.

This sign was only significant for me because Robert and I would playfully argue from time to time about whether these were called dragonflies or mosquito hawks, as I called them. He was right, of course—he always was, but we enjoyed the banter. The rainbows are very special gifts that I treasure, along with his many other messages.

The latest occurrence happened one day while I was sitting out on my patio. I had been agonizing over a decision that I had just made. Suddenly light danced across the floor in front of me as if to confirm the correctness of my decision. I looked behind me where there is just a blank wall and the blue sky above, but there was no logical reason for that lovely light.

Linda said that we should be expectant and open to receiving these signs and miracles. I'm not afraid of death or dying, because I know with all my heart that we live forever with love that never dies.

You cannot see what you do not look for.

I will share with you a humorous and heartwarming story about Kerry's experience with her deceased grandmother. I had known Kerry for several years, doing readings for her every few months, when she came to me after her grandmother had died. She was delighted to receive messages from her grandmother about joining Kerry's parents on the other side.

Kerry told me that she was going to Houston with her sisters to divide up her deceased grandmother's possessions. Her grandmother laughed and said she would be there with them and she would give them a sign. Because of her many obligations, Kerry had forgotten her grandmother's promise. While working in the house, Kerry and her sisters all began smelling something. Coming from an Italian family, they quickly recognized the tantalizing aroma of their grandmother's spaghetti sauce. They were unable to find a feasible source, as the aroma just wafted through the house, until Kerry remembered the promise. When she shared her grandmother's message with her sisters, they were all delighted with the gift of great memories their grandmother had brought to them from the other side, turning what would have been a difficult task into an afternoon of joyful laughter as they shared their memories of family get-togethers.

Kerry has since shared this letter with me:

> Linda, you told me to watch for signs, and they have continued to come. About three months ago, I came home and when I walked into my house, I again smelled spaghetti sauce for about fifteen minutes. The smell didn't travel around like it did in my grandmother's house, but nonetheless it was very strong. My stereo also comes on, but only at night, only when I am in bed, and never on the same station. I just turn it off and acknowledge my dad. He was definitely a music lover.
>
> I dream about all three: Mom, Dad, and my grandmother. Each time I wake up, I feel a little nostalgic, but now I don't wake up crying.

Just like you, I have my own doubts, insecurities, and fears. I certainly do not claim to understand how all of this metaphysical stuff works. It is a total mystery to me, but I just walk through each day with faith—faith in my spiritual support system to always be there for me, and faith that Spirit will work through me to help each and every person who comes to me to receive what they are searching for. Whether it is the healing energy that Spirit flows through me to heal a physical or emotional problem, or words of guidance and support from their angels and guides, or messages of healing from their loved ones in spirit, I trust that all of this and more will come from Spirit. I have stopped struggling to understand it; I just trust and accept that it all comes from a place of unconditional love, the heart of God. My favorite part of this wonderful job that God has given me is helping people who are grieving to heal.

As I've explained throughout this book, prior to Spirit awakening me to the gifts I had been given, I led a very average life and I still do, part of the time. I am a daughter, sister, wife, mother to two daughters and step-mother to two more daughters, as well as grandmother to five grandsons. My life is very similar to the lives of many of you, I am sure. I raised my family in a small town, being room-mother at my daughters' school and chauffeur to my children's many activities. When my eighteen-year mar-riage fell apart, it was just the beginning of an undeniable transformation of my life. My normal life was soon to change, and I had no idea how much. The drastic transformation from a life that was 100 percent normal to doing what some people consider really weird was difficult for many in my family to understand. I certainly don't blame them. As I said before, I don't always understand it myself. I've had to accept that Spirit has a plan for me, just as he has for you. My family soon began to learn more about the gifts I was working with, and their acceptance has meant a lot to me.

My sister-in-law was one of the last people I would have expected to believe any of this, because she is always so logical in her thinking, but her deceased father was pretty adamant in convincing her. Only her words can describe her experience.

To be honest, I never thought I'd be telling this story to anyone, because I never thought something like this could happen. Let me provide some history on myself. I'm a middle-aged professional woman working in the high-tech industry and have always consid-ered myself extremely logical and analytical, always approaching new ideas and concepts from a scientific view—needing to prove to myself what is real. I was raised by a very intelligent, dynamic, yet domineer-ing and extremely controlling father who was a pilot in the Air Force. I guess you could say that ego might have been his middle name, or at least that's what lots of people saw. I think you have to have that to be able to do his job. I saw it as a high level of confidence.

When I was twenty-seven, my dad passed away after a yearlong struggle with lung cancer. Of course, I'm sure the two-pack-a-day smoking habit probably had something to do with it, but nevertheless it was devastating for me to lose my father. He was the foundation and rock that I had built my life around, always providing excellent guidance and direction to me, always a role model for me to mirror my professional life against. Even though I was a female, he always expected me to forge my own path and excel and lead in the highly competitive, male-dominated high-tech world. I believe he was very proud of all of my accomplishments, although he was not one to give praise. When he passed away, I had a two-year-old daughter (who was the love of his life), and I was one month pregnant with another child. After his death, I was completely devastated about my loss and felt extremely short-changed. My marriage struggled, and five years later we divorced.

A few years later I married a very warm, loving man, who has to this day given me outstanding support and unconditional love. He has helped provide loving guidance to both of my daughters through some extremely difficult custody battles. To this day, I cannot imagine what I would have done if I had not met this man. He has enabled me to see the world in a very different light. But even though we have a strong relationship, I continued to feel a deep emotional gap in my life. I could never put a finger on what was causing it, and given it had been so many years since my father's death, I assumed that I had recovered from my loss.

Over the last five years, I have watched my sister-in-law develop an ability to—okay, I cannot believe I am going to say this—"talk to dead people." Needless to say, I have never been one to believe in talking to folks who have died. My view has been that's for the emotional dreamers and folks who have a great imagination. I do believe in God, but it was always my analytical view that I need to have hard physical proof to believe in something. Then an event happened that completely changed my perspective. I talked to my dad. Actually, to be accurate, I talked to my sister-in-law, who passed along my dad's words to me. Why and how did I know it was him? Well, the why is harder for me to explain, but since the reading with my dad, I have realized that there were a number of events that led me to talk to him.

For the last few years, I had continued to feel a deep emptiness, and although we had beautiful, talented daughters and my husband and I were proud of and involved in all their activities, I questioned why I never felt happy or at ease. There had always been a sense of dissatisfaction and a questioning of why I was not happy or ful-filled even with a beautiful family and great career. I do not feel like I ever enjoyed my life or family like I should—you know, living in the moment. A few years ago, my husband almost died of a rather rare condition, and my sister-in-law was instrumental in keeping our spirits up and, even then, bringing a spiritual element to his recovery, even though I never acknowledged that this had anything to do with his recovery. He is now handling his condition very well and continues to work and maintain a happy perspective on life.

Several months later, I had started working on a needlework project, something I enjoy doing for relaxation, when I felt compelled to tell my husband that I wanted to do an angel needlework stitching for his sister. When I talked to my husband about what I wanted to do, I was showing him a stitching kit catalog and pointed out several angel kits. For some reason, he pointed out a kit that was an angel holding a dove, but the really odd thing about the design was that the angel was clothed in a patriotic-style dress, with coloring like a U.S. flag on a background with the words of the Declaration of Independence—not exactly the type of design I *ever* would have considered doing. It made very little sense to me . . . a patriotic angel?? I had a compelling desire to finish it in time to frame it and give it to my sister-in-law for Christmas. I felt a lot of pride when I gave it to her, although I was afraid she'd question the patriotic theme as much as I had. She did not, and loves it and has it displayed in her office.

Shortly after Christmas, she and my husband had a shared birthday celebration, and afterward we were chatting on the couch. The topic came around to her work. I knew she stayed very busy doing readings for clients. During our discussion, I mentioned that I was interested in having a reading with her to try to talk to my dad. Did I really believe in this? Not really, but thought it would be interesting to just hear what she had to say. Of course, she knew nothing about my father, as it had never been a topic of conversation and he had passed away long before my husband and I met. While my husband had seen pictures of my dad, he also knew very little about my father. When I mentioned to my sister-in-law that I wanted to do a reading with my father, she paused and immediately asked me what he had to do with airplanes. I was shocked! She didn't know anything about his life and career as a pilot. I was startled and then told her he had been an Air Force pilot. She said that when I mentioned my father, she saw an airplane quickly flash across her view. When I told her that I really wanted to do a reading with her, she told me that he was ready. I was caught off-guard, but all these emotions just welled up inside of me. I couldn't stop thinking about this episode for weeks.

A few weeks later, my sister-in-law agreed to do a reading with me, so we sat down together, tape recorder on, and I started talking with my dad. How do I know it was him? There were so many references to things in our lives that I *know* my sister-in-law knew nothing about that I could not imagine it being anyone else besides him. He talked about our lives growing up and how difficult and controlling he was. He talked about my sisters and their personalities, some of them completely unknown to my sister-in-law. He talked about my daughters and my first husband, describing him and their personalities to a T. He told me that he was the one who sent the airplane flying across my sister-in-law's view, trying to communicate with me with a symbol he knew I would recognize. He also described his career. Throughout our reading, the words he used and the manner in which they were said were clearly the way he used to talk to me. Believe me, it was nothing like how my sister-in-law talks. I let my mom listen to a lot of the taped reading later, and the entire time he was describing our family life and the relationships and issues we had, she was shaking her head yes. She was convinced that this was my dad, speaking to us.

Later, in a separate session for my youngest daughter, he described red shoes that she used to wear. Interestingly, she didn't remember them, but when she mentioned it to me and my husband, we both instantly remembered a pair of red cowboy boots that she used to wear constantly until they no longer fit. She used to dance around in those boots. Even my mom remembers those red boots. My sister-in-law never saw her in those boots or any pictures with her wearing the boots.

Immediately following my reading, I went home, emotionally drained. I shared my unbelievable experience with my daughter later that evening. While talking with her, I continued to cry, something I felt I had been doing all day. My sister-in-law called me right at that moment. She called to tell me that he told her he wasn't done and wanted her to tell me to stop crying. I was absolutely shocked. So was my daughter. During the week after my reading, I felt an overwhelming sense of joy. I cannot explain it, but my outlook on life and on people had changed. That void I had felt for years was fading.

I am now convinced that my dad finally found a way to speak to me and give me advice and comfort after all those years. I am also convinced that if I had gone to any other person besides my sister-in-law, whom I had known for over ten years, I would not have been able to accept the words or believe in the concept at all. The stitching I did for her? After our reading, I spent a few weeks continuing to think about everything that led me to my reading, and a light bulb went off in my head—the stitching I did was patriotic, yet an angel. My sister-in-law loves angels. It never crossed my mind that the patriotic flag aspect of the design represented everything my dad stood for as an American Air Force pilot. I do not even begin to understand how we can talk to the spirits, but when this realization hit me, I paused and asked my dad if this patriotic angel was meant to help me establish the connection, and everything came back loud and clear—yes. I now have a picture of this design on my wall. For some reason, I actually took a picture of the needlework I did before I gave it to her. I think I know why now.

I am on a road of discovery at this point. The emptiness I have felt inside is beginning to be healed, although I understand that this will be a long learning process. My dad has always been there for me during my most difficult times, and I know he's with me now. Being the analytical, scientific person that I am, I continue to question everything and look for proof. I listen to the tape of my reading over and over again. I have started to read every book I can get my hands on and have started talking to people around me, albeit a little bit nervously because I really don't want to appear "wacky" or illogical. All I do know is that I've started on a journey of discovery, and this is the beginning of my healing process, not the end. My entire outlook on life has changed, and I have Linda and my dad to thank for this. I only hope that others have the opportunity to experience what I did.

I have become very accustomed to the unusual things that happen all around me, causing me to sometimes overlook the important messages that are right in front of my face. Our intuitive gifts are gifts to be used to help others. They can seldom be used to foresee events in our own lives, but, just like you, I am given messages from my spirit guides. That is why psychics or intuitives reach out to other psychics for guidance. As for myself, I may have received a message from my guides or a strong intuition about my life, but I appreciate confirmation or clarity. This is the same with most other mediums or psychics.

My stepdaughter, Heather, and her family moved from Arizona to be closer to our family. It wasn't long after moving into their house that things started happening. The lights in the dining room would flicker, eventually turning off and on by themselves regularly. Light bulbs throughout the house were continually blowing out. Her husband checked one particular fixture for obvious wiring shorts and replaced the switch, but to no avail. Heather had an unexplainable feeling that it was her Granddaddy Charlie, even though he had been gone nearly twenty years. When I asked Spirit who was in the house, I received confirmation that yes, it was him. They accepted his presence. The light fixture he repeatedly played with inexplicably fell from the ceiling one day when no one was home. His explanation was that it was dangerous and he needed someone to pay attention to it. He continued to flicker the lights to announce his presence. He had been around for about eight months, during which time my mother-in-law, Emma, had suffered through many health challenges. The connection with his timely presence did not dawn on me until she had a severe stroke and I saw him in her hospital room. How could I have been so blind? He knew she was leaving, and he was there waiting to assist her across. They had experienced a wonderful relationship together while on earth. Because of severe arthritis, she had gotten to the point that she was ready to leave and prayed daily to be released from the burden of this life. We didn't dare make funeral plans for fear that she would be asking daily, "Can I go now?" After a debilitating stroke, she made the choice to let go. She felt it was God's answer to her prayers. It was difficult for all of us observing her experience, even though she was so looking forward to her impending transition. We knew there would be a huge hole left in our hearts and lives.

As I sat by her bedside each day, watching her body slowly loosen its grip on life, she shared with me all of the people she saw filling her room. She talked about glowing images of angels, her husband, Charlie, and even her mother, who had died when she was young. As she vividly described them, she delighted in the fact that I too saw them. We talked about her memories as she saw an elderly couple that had befriended her as a child come into the room and wave to her. These were all souls that had come from the other side to assist her across and welcome her home. After her death, I truly did not expect to hear from her, considering her excitement about going home to join Charlie.

But she returns every now and then, giving us messages. She even came through one time while I was giving someone else a message. This happened at a psychic fair, and the lady I was reading for was also an intuitive. She stopped me in mid-sentence, saying that I was too modest to accept Emma's words of thanks to me, so Emma was speaking through her to thank me and say how much she loved me. I treasured the message, even though I had heard her say it many times. It was confirmation that, yes, I am truly hearing her.

One year after Emma's death, my husband took me to a restaurant for lunch. We had celebrated Emma's last birthday there just before her death but hadn't been back since. Her party had been a huge family gathering that we all had enjoyed. Returning to the restaurant stirred up many memories. While walking across the parking lot, I felt something hit me on the head and drop off my shoulder. I looked to the ground to find a penny. I looked around, but there was no one there but us. I picked up the penny and put it in my pocket to examine later. That next morning while I was meditating, Emma came to me. I recognized her mischievous giggle. She thanked me for the party I had given her and all the special things I had done for her. She laughed about the penny but said it was all she had to get my attention. I went looking for the penny that I had placed in my pocket. I smiled when I saw the date on it, 2003, the year she had died. I have heard of pennies from heaven, so I suppose there must be a big pot of pennies that they use to remind us that they are around us. By the way, we haven't seen any trace of Granddaddy Charlie since Emma left. He had come to walk home with her, and they are together again in bliss.

Sometimes we find ourselves racing through life so fast that we forget that Spirit has a plan for us. We created that plan for our life with Spirit's help. The support system that God gave us assists us as we make our way through the experiences of our plan. Everything that happens in our lives is part of that plan. God just helps us fit the puzzle pieces of our lives together. Even though Angel Darlin', in our next story, walks her spiritual path, in times of desperation she forgets to trust and remember there is a plan. Here is the story of her experience with the love of her life.

> This is the story of Hubba Bubba and Angel Darlin'. We were together for seven short years until H.B. passed away from cancer. We both knew that this was the contract between us before we came back to the planet and that Spirit was guiding our lives. Many miracles happened during these times and continue even today, as H.B. is helping me from the other side.
>
> For New Year's 1996, H.B. asked Spirit to bring him his next lesson. It came in the form of "his" redhead. He had been seeking his next right mate since his divorce fourteen years prior, and knew he would "know" her on the spot. He met a psychic at a local bookstore, and she asked him out. They ended up at a New Age networking dinner on January 20.

At the same time, a girlfriend and I made Treasure Maps for New Year's Eve. I asked for a relationship "fit for a queen," and I had recently "feng shui-ed" my junk closet in order to manifest a great new love. She and I attended the New Age networking dinner as well.

Attendees received playing cards that represented their lives. Mine was a 2 of Clubs and came with a computer printout predicting that I would marry the 8 of Clubs within the next few months. (Oh, right!) H.B. had the 8, and was seeking the 2 for the same outcome. Although he was there on a date with another woman, when we met that night we each recognized the other immediately, and we both knew our spirit guides were hard at work. Since then, I have believed in love at first sight.

Also that evening, one of the local psychic jewelers received a message to gift me with a crystal necklace of drusy cobaltite (a pink stone that draws in one's mate), which I had admired for months. She had been unable to sell the piece all through the holidays, and discovered that it was a gift to me from the universe.

H.B. and I ran into each other again the next day at a psychic fair at a local bookstore, but he was still with the "other woman." After about ten days, he finally called to ask me out, as he had determined that I wasn't going to call him. He said he felt like he was in the seventh grade, because he hadn't asked anyone for a date since his divorce, since all the women called him. He was surprised and relieved when I said, "Yes, of course." We went out for burgers and talked and talked and talked some more. He never went home, and we felt like we were still on our first date until the day he died.

While he was on a business trip in Orlando that February, I casually looked at rings. He was so psychic that he knew, immediately. He had me describe each ring over the phone. He made the selection with the help of his spirit guides, and he called the jeweler to have it sized. On Valentine's Day, the jeweler called me to pick up what turned out to be my engagement/wedding ring. Upon my arrival at the store, the jeweler called H.B., who happened to be in his hotel room. H.B. asked me to marry him and gave me the ring, with the jeweler as the "stand-in" to put it on my finger. You know, I just now realized that this was set up by Spirit ahead of time!

Although our families and friends were aghast that we had known each other for such a short time, we married in April, never suspecting that a year later H.B. would be diagnosed with malignant colon cancer. On our first anniversary, he had a foot of his colon removed.

Although the doctors recommended chemotherapy, H.B. declined because of ambiguous test results, and we went back to our "normal" lives. About twelve months later, he was feeling less and less energetic, and finally realized that something was drastically wrong.

By then we had moved from Houston to the Texas Hill Country. I had lost my job and health insurance, and H.B. was self-employed but not really working, so we had no funds for doctors. He was seen by a local naturopath who diagnosed a liver problem and then sent him to a doctor in San Antonio for another colonoscopy at a much-reduced fee. Although the colonoscopy was clear, this doctor was able to tell that there was something unusual about the liver, which was enlarged to the size of a basketball.

I got a job in San Antonio but still had no health insurance, and this was in the days of preexisting conditions. As it turned out, one of my new co-workers was the grandmother of the San Antonio liver transplant poster-boy, and another of my co-workers had just completed a business transaction with the head of the liver transplant team at the University of Texas Health Science Center. So H.B. visited with this doctor, who could not imagine how in the world he had ended up in his office without a physician's referral. After a reduced-rate MRI, which confirmed that the cancer had metastasized into the liver, he was told that they would not consider him a good candidate for a transplant, and referred him to a local oncologist.

That doctor was one of God's angels on earth. He was very upfront with H.B. He told him that he had about six weeks to live if he did nothing, and that there were no guarantees, but chemotherapy might reduce the liver tumors and enable him to have a couple more good years. H.B. explained our financial circumstances, but this doctor was not interested in money—he had made plenty and felt like he could afford to "give back" through pro-bono treatment. After a referral to a local hospital, which provided free liver tests, H.B. started chemotherapy and shaved his head as a sacrifice to the "chemo gods."

As the chemo made him more and more ill and unable to drive, I was able to leave my office to take him to the doctor each week, and make up my missed time on Saturday mornings. I was in exactly the right job situation to deal with this. What a blessing.

During this touch-and-go period, H.B. applied for and received emergency ninety-day turn-around Social Security disability benefits, which were retroactive back a couple years. Another major miracle! With the proceeds, we purchased a lovely home in San Antonio

toward the end of 1998, and had H.B.'s mother over from Missis-
sippi for a visit. While she was with us, we had a plumbing problem between the washing machine and main bathroom line, and
the plumbers sent by the warranty company told us that we had a
cracked slab in our new house. They said the maximum they would
pay for this type of problem was $500, and the check was in the
mail.

We then had the insurance adjuster look at this issue, and he sent
over the plumbing company he used for this type of circumstance.
These guys were great. First, they determined that there were two
separate sets of lines beneath the house—the snake-deal put in at
the washing machine drain would never come out at the opposite
bathroom since they were never connected in the first place. So there
was no cracked slab. The camera sent into the water lines determined
there were some roots clogging up the pipes, so they replaced about
five feet of PVC pipe at no charge once they realized H.B.'s health
situation.

That same week, I was laid off from my job! Big bummer! A week
later I was working for one of the largest employers in San Antonio,
with full health insurance coverage for H.B., with no maximum dol-
lar limit on cancer treatment. After having received over $350,000 of
free treatment, he was thrilled to make a $15 co-pay each week once
the insurance went into effect. Another situation that had looked like
a tragedy on the surface turned out to be a miracle.

The following year Medicare kicked in to supplement the insurance coverage. The treatments were difficult, but H.B. was a star patient,
and made a huge commitment to do everything the doctor suggested.
Based on his own research, H.B. did some complementary non-allopathic
protocols as well. The doctor was very open-minded and interested in
all the research that was done. And by the year 2000, H.B. was feeling
better—walking four miles per day and maintaining a few computer
clients, even occasionally traveling out of town to work on their systems.

We knew he was going to die and had talked about the subject at
great length. Because Hubba Bubba loved San Francisco, I suggested
that his twin sons and I would place his cremated remains in the Bay
after his death. So that year he took the three of us to California for a
vacation and showed us his favorite place, where he wanted his ashes
sprinkled, behind the Veteran's Memorial Golf Course, overlooking

where the Pacific Ocean goes into the Bay, which has a breathtaking view with the Golden Gate Bridge in the background.

After that trip, his health went into another gradual decline. Dr. A. suggested a treatment where the chemo was placed directly into the liver by some sort of surgical procedure. H.B. was getting weaker, and after a few of these, they decided to try inserting a chemo pump directly into the liver. And this one saved his life, as there was gangrene from the prior surgeries, adhering the appendix and the gall bladder together—the surgeon was able to remove all the dead tissue and insert the pump, which worked only once. We knew this was yet another miracle.

However, his health went into even more of a decline. As he could no longer drive, our housekeeper, who is another of God's angels on earth, took H.B. to and from chemotherapy each week, and we spent every Sunday morning at the weekend lab getting "fluffed," which is the nickname for inserting a couple of bags of fluids into the chemo patient to perk them up. Although the doctors told him there was not much more they could do, Dr. A. and H.B. got their heads together and came up with their own experimental combinations, hoping to find a treatment protocol that would eventually help other patients with similar issues.

Eventually Dr. A. told H.B. to call hospice to come to the house to take care of him, because there was no more that could be done. I took him to see the doc that had meant so much to him one last time, to tell him "thank you, goodbye, and God bless." H.B. lasted another six weeks.

During these six weeks, my brother Mac called to say he had been driving across the desert in New Mexico when H.B.'s spirit "came by" and rode around with him and talked to him. At that time, H.B. made a commitment to look after Mac's two young daughters once H.B. reached the other side. Mac's daughter Jenny, at that time five years old, walked into H.B.'s room and said, "You know, Uncle H.B., sometimes people just go ahead and die in their sleep." All she knew is that he was ill—so how did this little girl come up with this? She says her angels told her. And now, two years later, we ask her how she slept, and she says just fine, she was out flying around with Uncle H.B. And she always wins at Sorry and Monopoly, because Uncle H.B. is helping her.

Also prior to his death, a friend called to say that H.B.'s spirit came in her patio door, swept all the books and magazines off the piano bench, and walked back out! He had given her a crystal a couple of years prior to this time, and she received a message from him that it was time to pass it along to me.

The hospice nurse came and got me early one morning after Thanksgiving and said, "Come quick! He's going now." I walked into the room and grabbed his hand. He opened one eye, gave me a wink and a grin, and was gone. What a gift!

We had made an agreement that once he passed over, H.B. would send me a signal from the other side to let me know he was around and could communicate with me. This signal was that the Plumerias would bloom. I had owned these plants for many years, and they rarely bloomed. Since his passing, they have bloomed profusely both summers!

Just prior to going to San Francisco to sprinkle his ashes in the Bay, I walked out of the house one morning, and the Texas Laurel trees were in full bloom—they had never bloomed much in the previous five years that we owned the house. And in the back yard, the roses were glorious. I pulled the petals off all the roses and took them with me to California, knowing full well that he had manifested the blossoms. And of course, the Plumeria were blooming as well.

H.B.'s twin sons, his ex-wife, and I met up in San Francisco on what would have been his fifty-fifth birthday to sprinkle his ashes into the Bay, as requested. There were about thirty people at the spot when we arrived, and they all left within two minutes. Amazing! I could see sparkling colors with every handful of ashes and rose petals as they caught in the wind.

H.B. can and does communicate from the other side. Just this past week, another friend noticed that he came by to check on things, and his sons see him occasionally. My brother noticed him checking on our home in San Antonio from about one hundred feet above the roof line several times before I sold the house. I have seen him in the armchair in my home and talk to him frequently. Plus, a lady at the Austin Psychic Fair reads for me, and it is always a message from H.B. My niece, now seven, sees him and communicates with him daily.

I am convinced that our situation and his health issues were all preordained and manifested exactly the way we wrote the script before coming back to the planet. I am also convinced that he is watching over me, helping me from the other side with my life's purpose as a healer, teacher, and channeler, becoming more tuned in every day to my spirit guides and angels.

Thank you, dear Hubba Bubba, for all you taught me and teach me still. I love you and miss you every single day. Love, Your Angel Darlin'.

When We Open Our Hearts, There Is So Much to Receive from Our Loved Ones in Spirit

Here is another story about how our loved ones can bring us comfort from the other side.

A few days after my father died, we were having family members over to decide on arrangements for the funeral. My mother and I were sitting in the foyer away from other family members when she mentioned that she wanted to hire an expensive florist from Houston who had an amazing reputation, and regardless of the cost, she wanted the best. I pointed out to my mother that she was very talented in arranging flowers and had been doing gorgeous arrangements for years at her church, and that Dean would probably prefer someone who loved him to arrange the flowers and save her the ridiculous expense. She looked at me, as her eyes teared up, and said that she didn't think she could do as good an arrangement as she believed he deserved. At that moment I was aware of my father standing beside her and I said, "He wants *you* to do them. He's here right now." She started to cry, saying she knew that he was, though she couldn't see him. I told her to ask for guidance while she arranged the flowers and they would be perfect. She shook her head yes and said, "Of course, I'll have so-and-so help me, and I will have a dozen long-stem red roses in the arrangement." I saw my father nodding in agreement. She agreed to do the flowers, and I watched my father pat her hands, which were folded in her lap. Then he looked at me and said, "Thank you, Nancy." That was the only time I saw my father after his death (it freaked me out a little bit), but it was a very important gesture. My mother and her friend did the flowers for the funeral, and they were spectacular, sporting a dozen long-stemmed red roses in the mix. Everyone commented on how stunning the flowers were, and my mother was overjoyed with the outcome.

chapter seven

Embracing God's Gift of Healing Our Pain

Sometimes tremendous healing can come from just a few words. Often when we lose a loved one, their absence can leave such a gaping hole in our hearts that we feel we cannot possibly go on with our lives, but just knowing that they are happy and in a loving place can bring us great comfort.

Most of the time when someone comes to me for an appointment, I don't know at the beginning of the session what they need, and sometimes neither do they, but Spirit always knows how to meet those needs. Spirit knows their heart and soul and what they need to experience to fill that empty place within them.

Here is an example of how our spirit guides lead us down our path to healing. I cherish the many letters I receive from grateful clients. This is one I will share with you.

My son was killed on April 5, 2003. It was the worst pain I've ever known. That night as I lay in bed trying to sleep, I started feeling waves of heat going up my body from my feet to my head. Over the next few days, that kept happening. I began to realize that it was my son, James, letting me know he was still here with me. Sometimes I would smell his cologne, or feel a touch on my arm or a squeeze on my hand. He gave me the support I needed to get through the funeral and, a year later, to get through the trial of the man that murdered him. Every time I felt the intense pain of losing him, I felt him squeeze my hand. Even though I knew he was still with me, it wasn't enough. I needed to know that he was okay.

Our town was having an event one weekend, and I saw in the newspaper that they were having someone doing spiritual psychic readings. I just knew I had to go. That's how I found you. You put your hands on mine and the first thing you said was, "Did you lose a son?" You told me that he was standing beside me and every time I cry, he cries with me. He said he was sorry for what we had to go through, but he's where he has to be. It was his time and he understands now why this happened. He told you that I don't smile anymore, and he wants to see me smile again. He said he's in paradise and it's beautiful there. He thanked me for all the times I helped him, and now he is helping me.

Even though I will never get over the pain of losing him, it gives me comfort to know that he is at peace and happy. That makes me happy. I've known people who lost children, but until it happens to you, it is impossible to understand that pain. It never goes away, but over time, day by day, it gets a little easier. I see and feel signs of his presence all the time. This has made me open my eyes and look. The more I look, the more I see. It hurts that I'll never again see him walk through the door or pick up the phone and hear him say, "What's goin' on?" But it also helps me to know that he will always be with me, and every day he lets me know that. Even though we were always close, in some ways I feel closer to him now than I ever did before.

I am quite honored that some of my clients bring their family and friends to experience Spirit's healing messages. Their trust is the greatest compliment on our work.

This is a letter I received from a longtime client:

Linda, I can't thank you enough for the many things you have done for me and my family. I was telling my mother about the information that you shared with my friend Carol from her deceased daughter (when her deceased daughter had to speak to her rather than letting you just do Reiki). Something really touched my mother. She started crying and said, "I have to see this woman." My mother is such a conservative, devout Catholic that I was surprised by this. While visiting here, we got the chance to have an appointment with you. During her appointment, I just sat over in the corner, while she was on the massage table for Reiki. My mother had only been on the table a moment when you walked over to me and very quietly asked if she would be "open" to receiving messages, too. I said, "Sure." You then told my mother that there was a man at the end of the table, and that you felt he was her father. He really wanted to tell my mother how sorry he was that he had pushed her so hard. You relayed to her that he said he had thought he needed to push her to make her strong for all of the things that she would have to deal with in life, but now he saw he had been wrong in doing so. You then elaborated about why he had felt he needed to make her strong.

You mentioned that he had experienced many deaths and losses when he was young. You went on to elaborate about those deaths: his father, two babies (very young), and a family pet. I was sitting there listening and learning. My mother said that he was her father and referred to the babies as "the twins." Her parents had lost twin babies at birth before she was born. My mother had tears in her eyes and seemed to be so pleased. My deceased grandfather continued to give you information for my mother, one thing after another, which she confirmed.

After the session, my mother walked out of the front door, immediately turned to me, and said, "Your father needs to come here."

When I brought my sister Lora to see you, and she was on the table receiving a Reiki session, you told her there were several women in spirit form that were standing around her. One of the women was carrying a rose. You said that she seemed like she might have passed recently because she wasn't really communicating, just tracing the letter *R* in the air. My sister and I both started crying. Our Aunt Rose had recently passed. You said that she said she was so happy, she sings all the time now. Rose had a wonderful singing voice, and after her cancer treatments in the last several years of her life she wasn't able to sing. She really missed it. All of the family, including Rose's children, were especially comforted by the messages you gave us that day.

I have such a great appreciation for your gifts that I am always eager to bring my friends and family to share you with them.

Healing Your Grief

We have addressed what grief is, but how do we heal it? With the loss of a loved one, it is greatly helpful to have a better understanding of death and the other side. We have already discussed the grief of losing a loved one, but what about the gaping hole their death has left in our lives? You have to accept that they are no longer with you in physical form, but your friend or loved one is still around you, and you can continue to have access to them on a spiritual level. If this gives you comfort, you can ask their spirits to be with you as you go through the grieving process. Talk with them as if they were sitting beside you. They will be there to listen to you and support you with their energy and prayers as you experience the many emotions of grief. If you do not feel comfortable talking to them, you can write them a letter, expressing all that you feel may have been left unsaid. Also, keeping a journal is very helpful, as sometimes it is easier to write about emotions when we are unable to talk about them. Stuffing and suppressing your emotions is not the answer, and neither is denying them. God did not create us as pillars of stone (strength). We are flesh and blood humans with feelings and emotions. We were created in God's own image, loving and compassionate, so how can we fault ourselves for having these emotions? Give yourself time to understand what you are feeling and why you are feeling it, as this is part of healing. Write about where you are with your grief each day, as that is a great gauge of your progress. Whether talking or writing, through expressing yourself, the numbness will subside and eventually you will begin to feel alive again.

An important part of healing your grief is forgiveness. Whether the issue involves forgiving yourself or forgiving your loved one, sincere forgiveness can give you the freedom to heal your grief and move forward with your life. Sometimes we are unable to find the answers to what is holding us in the depths of our grief. As painful as it is, this is the time that we must examine our past relationship with our loved one much more closely, as we look for the answers. Many of you hold painful memories of abuse, neglect, or abandonment with a parent, child, spouse, or friend. Examine the history between you and how it can be addressed and forgiven. You and your loved one deserve to be free of any negative emotions or karma that may still exist between you. This is done through truthful soul-searching and forgiveness. Otherwise, those negative emotions will continue to create blockages in your life, preventing you from achieving success, happiness, and fulfillment in your relationships and careers.

Often, to achieve this healing, you may need help. Don't allow your painful negative emotions to deny you the happiness you deserve. You may obtain this help through professional counseling, clergy counseling, or intuitive life-path healers such as myself.

The Grief of an Anticipated Death

Alzheimer's disease is a progressive condition in which nerve cells degenerate in the brain. The cause is unknown at this time.

Alzheimer's disease is a slowly progressing form of dementia. It causes progressive impairment of intellectual function, greatly affecting cognitive thought and memory, as well as diminished functioning of motor skills. It has three stages. A person with the disease can live five to twenty-five years. Toward the end, everything in the person's body stops functioning.

Those are the clinical facts about Alzheimer's; this is the reality of how it affects a life, a marriage, and a family. This is Dorothy's experience with the loss of her husband, Joe, to Alzheimer's disease.

My husband, Joe, was a mail carrier in our rural community and had a 108-mile route every day except Sunday. He mentioned to me that he was concerned because he was having a problem putting the mail in the right box. I didn't think much about it at the time, as everyone makes mistakes. Joe came home one day and told me he was going to have to retire. Thinking he had just had enough of his mail route, I supported his decision. Then, day after day, I started to notice something was wrong. Joe was becoming more and more confused. It seemed as though overnight our lives began to fall apart. When the doctors diagnosed Alzheimer's, my heart sank. I feared even thinking about what our future would hold. Our love was strong, but my fear of the unknown kept creeping in. We had been married for twenty-four years. Our life together hadn't been easy, but we had embraced every moment of it. We both enjoyed our fishing trips to the coast, recently dreaming and planning for our retirement together. We had each taken on the responsibility of caring for our respective ailing mothers. At the beginning, neither of us understood the amount of work that would entail or the lack of family support we would receive. This commitment had involved taking care of them as best we could prior to putting them in nursing homes when Joe became unable to help me. They each remained there through most of Joe's illness.

Joe's condition progressed so quickly that I moved from denial to reality in one short step. I felt a great responsibility to take care of my husband and give him the kind of loving care he deserved. I was strong and sure that our love would get us through this, as it had in the past. In my times of doubt, I kept repeating that belief. I didn't have time to worry about what the future would bring, because the present was all-consuming.

After Joe's retirement, I had to continue to go to work each day, constantly worrying about what he was doing at home. I realized Joe's condition was worsening when I received a call from the bank saying that he had cashed a check for $500. I went downtown to see if I could get him to come home. He ran from me . . . looking at me as if I were a stranger. A friend had to talk him into coming home. The emotional pain I would endure was only beginning. I tried to understand what was happening to Joe, but it was so hard not knowing what to expect next. Things got progressively worse. He became delusional, believing there were people outside our bedroom that were going to come in and kill us. He would never sleep at night but would walk back and forth, keeping me awake. Having to go to work with little or no sleep was pretty rough. Work actually became my escape, but then I began to feel guilty for feeling that way. Joe was no longer rational, so how could I talk to him? I saw the man I loved slipping away very quickly, and there was nothing I could do. I felt so helpless. I longed for Joe, the husband I loved so much, to return to me, to love me the way he had throughout our marriage.

That was not to be, as our situation continued to worsen. There are two types of Alzheimer's patients: the meek, mild, childlike ones and the angry, abusive, aggressive ones. It became obvious that Joe was becoming the aggressive type.

Joe started going outside at night and roaming around. Knowing his condition, I knew he would get lost, so I had to lock the doors and hide the keys to protect him. This made him very angry. In Joe's fits of anger, he would strike out at me, frequently hitting me and knocking me to the floor. I found myself angry at the painful abuse I was enduring while trying to make excuses for his actions. I kept telling myself, this is not the man I loved; he would never do this to me. In one such incident, Joe knocked me to the floor. With a screwdriver in hand, he stabbed at me, at me, his wife, the one he had previously cherished so dearly. His anger had taken control of all of his senses. Being that he was so much stronger than I, my only defense was to bite his arm. Joe reeled in surprise at my action, but it gave me time to get away from him. I fought back tears of frustration and anger that I was having to fight for my life against this man whom I loved so much. I felt guilty for having to hurt him, and I fumed with anger at this disease that had taken my loving husband away from me.

It wasn't long after that episode that I had to call my brother-in-law to the house to help me because Joe had gotten his rifle out and was waving it around. I hadn't previously thought of the danger of the guns we kept in the house but quickly got rid of them. I even had to start locking my bedroom door after I awoke one night, feeling something was wrong. Joe was standing over me, just staring at me as if I were a stranger. To Joe, I had become a stranger, as he had to me. One night when he found the door was locked, he began to try breaking it down. I had to call friends to help me get him to the hospital for medication and observation. Hospitalization was not what I wanted for him, but I was at the end of my rope and realized he needed more help than I could give him. The doctor took one look at my bruises and said Joe could not come home.

I still had my husband, but I felt so alone. At times I would think back to our memories of the past, reminiscing about the trips we'd taken and being so thankful for the time we'd had together. I tried very hard not to be angry at what I had lost, but sometimes even the effort of trying was too much to handle. If you ever have a loved one with Alzheimer's disease, it will either make you very strong or break you. It is the worst disease you could possibly get. I had a husband in body, yet he was not there. It was as if the devil had possessed him. I thank God, as he was kind enough to give me the strength to get through this ordeal.

Once Joe's doctor got his medications adjusted, he put Joe in a nursing home. His disease progressed quickly. I would go each day to visit him and take him outside in his wheelchair, and sometimes we would laugh together, but it was obvious he didn't know who I was. I brought him his favorite foods so I could sit and feed him, but it was really more for my sake because he had retreated to the point that he didn't know what was going on. I felt so helpless, but by then he was probably in the third stage of the disease.

One day when I came to the nursing home, he was sitting in his chair waiting for someone to feed him. He looked up at me, reached out his arm, gave me a big smile, and wanted a kiss. I looked in his eyes and actually saw my Joe. I knew this was God working through him, giving me the chance to say goodbye, as he let me know the end was near. The state Joe was in, he would never have been able to do this on his own, and God had given me a glimpse of my Joe again. With me by his side day and night, he passed away on December 23, 1996.

With Alzheimer's disease, grieving the loss of your loved one begins long before the physical body passes. Frequently the grief and long-term trauma of the experience are carried within you for the rest of your life. This is why finding a method of healing this grief is so important.

chapter eight

Preparing for Death: The Stages of Dying and Death

When you are faced with the imminent loss of a loved one, it is always a painful experience, even when you are given time to prepare. Communication with this person prior to their death makes it so much easier for both of you to accept and proceed on the journey of the soul's path. Our loved one may be holding on to their life force long past the human body's ability to sustain any quality of life.

This sometimes occurs when the person has a feeling of responsibility to those being left behind, for example a mother who can't bear the thought of leaving her children (whether small or grown) because she knows they have depended on her all of their lives. She will grip life with white knuckles and endure the suffering to keep from abandoning her children. She sees how frightened the family is at the prospect of losing her. Even when we are adults, the loss of a parent is devastating. They are often our security, the shoulder we can cry on, the umbrella that shelters us from the hardships of life. When the rest of our life is in chaos, they are there for us. The thought of their absence in our lives can have indescribable emotions attached to it.

It is at this time that we must use all that they (our parents) have taught us and acknowledge the reality of the situation. We must be strong enough to walk through our own fears about death to become their (our parents') support system. It is necessary that we be clear and rational about recognizing that it is time for our loved one to pass. This is the greatest gift you can give your loved one as they prepare for their soul's journey.

I consulted with a close friend who is a chaplain doing "end of life" care at a hospital in Arizona. She shared with me a few of her experiences with terminal patients and how they faced their own death.

> Samantha entered the hospital with uncontrolled pain, nausea, and the inability to eat. Four weeks before, she had received a diagnosis of pancreatic cancer that had metastasized to the liver. The patient had had a mother and son both die from cancer. She also had been the caretaker of her husband, who had suffered with multiple sclerosis for many years. The present circumstances were difficult for the patient and her family.
>
> Samantha and her family struggled with the decision to enter hospice care. To them, hospice represented death, and the family members were not ready to accept that she was going to die. When I visited with Samantha, she explained her dilemma. She did not want to continue with the chemotherapy because of its side effects. She knew she was dying. She wanted to enter an in-house hospice program that would help control the pain, and then she wanted to go home to die. Those were her wishes, but she saw the fear in her family's eyes. They depended so much on her. Samantha's husband begged her to continue the chemo, because he needed her to live. He loved her dearly and admitted he didn't know how to face life without her. The family talked about it and wanted a miracle. The family stated that she had no symptoms to control; therefore she did not need hospice. Samantha struggled with her pain in order to hold on for her family. Finally, a doctor who was an expert in pain control was allowed to work with the patient. Within twenty-four hours, the symptoms had resolved to the point that Samantha could go home with hospice care, and she died shortly after. She was surrounded by her family, just as she had wanted.
>
> The dynamics of the situation involved unresolved grief about her husband's illness and the death of her mother and son. Samantha had accepted the terminal diagnosis, but the family had not. Her family put pressure on her to live for them because they could not deal with another loss, especially of someone they loved and needed so much.

They didn't want her to suffer, but they didn't want to face the truth either. She was in uncontrolled pain and not able to keep food down, but her family was looking to the chemotherapy to be their miracle because of their needs, not hers. In their fear and grief, they didn't realize what they were asking of her. Samantha had enormous guilt about dying and leaving her family, which made her decisions even more difficult.

Prayer is the most powerful tool God has given us. It is meant to be used throughout our lives, and it is especially powerful during challenging times such as these. Pray not just for the loved one preparing to pass but for the family as well. Ask for God's assistance to guide you through your loved one's passing and transition, giving you the strength to endure the challenges to come. Spirit explains to me that our prayers are helpful in ensuring that our loved one has a smooth transition along their soul's journey.

Communicating with Our Loved Ones

In my work, I have had the privilege of being part of the support system for many families as they faced the loss of a loved one. It is not easy for the family, but I have found that a tremendous amount of love and healing can come through open communication at this time. We all must grieve the loss of our loved ones. Through our loved one's journey toward death, we frequently begin experiencing our own grief even before the end has come. Communication can help you find joy in the time you have left together in your relationship.

Talk to your loved one about their life. Share the happy memories as well as the sad ones. That is what life is about. If you have pictures, utilize them to relive joyful events in your life. Be sure to write on the back of the pictures who these people are. Take notes and gather as much information as you can, as you will treasure what you have gained from them. If you have siblings, involve them in the healing process, as that is what it really is. Heal old wounds by using this opportunity to speak from your heart. A tremendous amount of karma can be healed during this time of saying goodbye. Allow yourself to be in a place of forgiveness for both yourself and your loved one.

If communicating through words of love is not comfortable in your relationship, this is a great time to learn how to express yourself. So many times I have heard, "If only I could have told them how much I loved them before they died." Use this time to learn and grow all you can through this experience, since that is what life is about. You may become a teacher for others; the next time someone around you must face the loss of a loved one, you can be there to assist them.

If your loved one seems to be stuck in a debilitated body with no quality of life left, one in which they are suffering, they may need your permission to leave or reassurance that you understand their need to leave, and that you will continue to love them as you heal from your loss.

These are words from Spirit, so I know them to be the truth.

Death is a gift from God, a reward given to us for all that we have endured in life, a transition to a new beginning.

There are many different stages of death, and most nurses, especially hospice nurses, are helpful in guiding you through these stages. As your loved one nears death, you will notice that they seem to be in and out of alertness. This is because their spirit is going in and out of their body. They are receiving guidance from their spiritual support group to prepare them for their transition. Even before their actual death, their spirit begins the transition process that allows them to begin healing any negativity created during their life.

At this time of grief, our emotions are so high that we often feel that they are pulling away from us. Our natural reaction is to want to touch them or hold their hand. While holding their hand may comfort us, it actually pulls them back into their body, slowing down their transition to the other world. It takes a lot of life force energy to make the transition from this world to the next. As you are touching them, they are using their life force energy to connect with you. I understand that you may want to show your love and support for them, but if possible please resist the urge to touch them. Their spirit hears you and finds great comfort in your words of love and support as well as your prayers assisting them on their journey.

This advice is directed toward the passing of a terminally ill person who is in the process of dying but is having difficulty physically letting go of their body. It is very difficult to be a part of someone's final moments of life. Our desire to comfort them and ourselves in this moment may override the knowledge that I have given you, and this is understandable. Just keep in mind that if someone is having difficulty with their final crossing, your touch may delay that crossing. It is your decision. Sometimes the emotional needs of those being left behind override the needs of the one dying, and this is understood by everyone involved.

As in the situation of the baby passing in chapter 3, the holding of the baby's hand is something the mother needed to be able to do to say goodbye and accept his death. The baby understood the mother's need to say goodbye and had no fear of death, so it was easy for him to pass. It is our fear of death that causes both the one passing over and the ones remaining here to struggle with the end-of-life experience.

Their soul is not leaving you; it is simply being released from a body that can no longer serve it. If it is *your* fear of death that is holding your loved one here past their time, you may be enveloped in a selfish love. This fear is understandable, but it is necessary that you get over it. That sounds harsh, and I don't mean it that way, but you do not want to hold your suffering loved one here because of your fears and insecurities. I have often seen the situation in which someone feels guilty that they didn't do enough for their loved one, or has regrets about a disagreement and feels they need to hold their loved one here for an opportunity to make amends. Or, they just plain fear that they cannot exist without that loved one. Talk it through, forgive yourself, forgive them, and heal the emotions so that you can let them go on their soul's journey. Don't try to ignore the inevitable death, as the situation will not go away; death is as natural as birth. I have found that resisting or denying your feelings only makes your inevitable emotions more intense and prolongs the grief. Death is a precious gift, given to us by a merciful God, a God who loves us and welcomes us home when it is our time. Our physical bodies were not meant to last for eternity; only our spirit bodies are given this promise.

Work through your issue with death and your impending loss. Keep in mind that your loved one is not abandoning you, but only releasing the bondage of their physical body. Ask for help from your angels and spirit guides. Read books, such as this one, that can give you a better understanding of death and grief. Seek counseling to help you through the process. We often need to receive this type of support even before our loss to help us proceed through a lengthy illness and impending death. Do not try to do it all on your own. Reach out to your support group, family, friends, priest, rabbi, or minister. There are also gifted chaplains in the hospitals to assist you. If you do not connect with one on an emotional level, search for another one.

I have a dear friend who is a chaplain at a local hospital. In using her love and compassion, she assists her patients on their soul's journey. She has agreed to share with us some of her experiences with those facing death. All names and personal details have been changed for privacy.

The Stages of Dying and Death

For some of you, this may be a difficult part to read, as it will give you the clinical perspective on death. For this information I went to my friend, Reverend Dolly, who is a beloved chaplain at a local hospital.

The reality is, we are all dying, and some of us just take longer than others. Most people are not afraid of death but are afraid of the dying process. That is because we have very limited information about it and how death occurs over a period of time. Each person's process is as unique as his or her fingerprints; however, there are patterns and signs that are similar and guide us in our efforts to help someone who is dying. The individual first goes through their own grieving process about no longer being here with friends and family. When there has been an acceptance that death will occur, the following signs become evident:

- Material items no longer hold the same value.
- Family, friends, and relationships are the priority.
- Unfinished business, including relationships, will receive more attention. It is the opportunity to heal old wounds and finish this round in love and acceptance of what is to come.
- Initially, the person will want to visit with those close to them, take trips that are meaningful, and do other things that have been put off.
- As the person gets closer to the active dying phase, they may withdraw into the womb of the home to conserve energy and to prepare for death. They may only want certain people to be around them. Others should not be offended by this. Just know that the use of energy is being protected. It is a natural part of the dying process. During this time, the individual may want to talk about the funeral and plan it, selecting clothing, casket, etc. It is a good thing for them to participate as much as possible. We tend to shy away from it, because it means we acknowledge the impending death and loss of a loved one.
- The individual may clean out drawers and closets.
- The individual may return items that have been given to them.

- The individual may talk of seeing and conversing with loved ones who have died. These spirits are there to help in the dying process and accompany them across the great divide between this world and the next.

The active dying phase consists of the following steps:

- Initially, the person will still be conscious and interactive. Over time, they will sleep more but can still be aroused. The individual will continue to accommodate the needs of the family. The person may be ready to leave, but the family may still have issues.

- Confusion and agitation may occur, characterized by thrashing around, picking at the covers, or restless movement. The person may describe seeing deceased loved ones in the room or appear to be having conversations with someone you can't see. (But just because a person is seeing spirits doesn't mean they are at death's doorstep!)

- Usually, pain is controlled through drugs. However, the person may not want to take the amount needed to control the pain because it makes them sleep more. They will want to be as alert as possible. Also, they may be afraid that they will not wake up.

- The person will reach a point where they do not want to eat or drink. The body can no longer absorb food or liquid. It will swell up and cause vomiting. But many times we have a need to continue to feed the person, because that is a sign that they are still very much alive and not leaving anytime soon. Our kindness makes the person very uncomfortable. They will not refuse to eat or drink because it is what we want. We tell them how they have to eat to keep up their strength, and they want to please us.

- Breathing goes through several phases, becoming very irregular and then going back to regular, and stopping at times. The person may stop breathing for forty-five seconds to one minute, sometimes longer, and then take a deep breath. The family will think the person has died, only to have them start breathing again. The final pattern of breathing is stressful, characterized by short, puffy breaths, until there is one final puff—this is the transition from life to death.

- The body temperature fluctuates between hot and cold. The person may be sweating profusely or feel really cold, because the brain is shutting down and the centers that control temperature no longer function. The body will begin to cool from the feet and hands inward, as blood pools toward the heart to keep it going. The body may take on a bluish tint.

- The coma is the final stage of the process. The person will not be aroused; however, they can still hear and feel touch. During this phase, the spirit is going back and forth between the body and the other side, getting ready to leave permanently. The person is engaging in spiritual work with God for the final leg of the journey. It is important to continue to talk to the person, giving them permission to leave. Families who hold on to the person make it difficult for them to complete the dying process. This phase can last several days to weeks. Families can become exhausted, because they have already been sitting vigil. It can be a very trying time for families, but they just have to stay the course. When the individual and God are both ready, the individual will exit.

- Some individuals will rally during part of the coma. They may wake up, be lucid, express final wishes and goodbyes, even ask for food and drink, but then enter the coma again. It is difficult for families, because they think the person has experienced a miracle and will get up and walk out of the hospital.

What I have just described is a situation with a person who is terminally ill. *If your loved one has not been diagnosed as terminally ill, the healing process is completely different.* It is important that you communicate with the doctors; ask a lot of questions, so that everyone is clear about what is really going on with your loved one, as well as what is needed from you for their healing. Whether your loved one has experienced injury or illness, your support is essential. They need all of the loving touch, communication, and prayer you can give them as healing support.

Taking Control of Your Future

It is important to know your loved one's wishes. Whether we are talking about spouses, parents, siblings, or grown children, it is important for others to know and understand what their wishes are about their life choices as well as their choice when it comes to death. This openness makes it so much easier for everyone involved to understand and accept the situation. The conversation may be uncomfortable, but it will take a lot of pressure off the family in the long run. If the decision has to be made for your loved one about giving or discontinuing life support, it is important that you know your loved one's wishes.

Many of us are put in exactly that situation with no preparation whatsoever. We must face the fact that we all are dying. From the moment of our birth, we begin the approach toward our transition into death. It is inevitable. Some of us have a control issue that causes us to want to have as much control as possible in our life right up until the end, so if that is your case, you had better get busy making your wishes known through a trust or will *and* an advance directive for physicians and family. This can be done through an attorney, or many hospitals offer advance directives and medical power of attorney paperwork for free. You just fill in your wishes, but be very specific. This is where an attorney can help if you do not know your options.

I have witnessed people being maintained on life support when there is no quality of life left, but unfortunately, the family members are not emotionally able to let go, or legally the doctors must keep them in this state of limbo. Sadly enough, I have actually seen and heard spirits such as these begging to be released. Life on the other side is too wonderful to be denied access. Think of the torture of being able to see and feel the beauty of a place as awesome as heaven but not be able to reach it because you are trapped in a shell of a body on earth. Spirits frequently use me to tell their families not to fear death. A physician's directive could prevent this situation. Both you and your family members over the age of eighteen need one. It is also important to have several copies, so that family members have access to it in case of emergency. Also, please consider and discuss with your family the possibility of organ donation. Your choice can give the gift of life to someone in need.

Here is my own experience. I knew the importance of a last will and testament, but I never knew the importance of an advance physician's directive, and a specific one, until my mother-in-law suffered a stroke. She had been wise enough to have a very thorough attorney draw up her will. Although I had heard the attorney quiz her about her wishes, I didn't realize the details that had been added to the standard directive until she began having health issues. The details of that advance physician's directive saved her from enduring a torturous experience as her body began its journey toward the end. Because of that physician's directive, she had a control over her life and death that few of us know much about. She was allowed to speed up her transition by refusing life-sustaining medical aid that would have prolonged her experience. The only way she could have done this was through the advance physician's directive prepared prior to her stroke. Bless her heart. As hard as it was for us to let her go, her journey to the other side was such a gift for her.

chapter nine

The Different Types of Losses

Our losses come in so many ways. In this chapter we will address the many different kinds of losses. My clients have been generous enough to share with us their experiences with death, grief, and the healing they experienced.

The Loss of a Parent

When I first began working with Linda, my mother was in the final stages of emphysema, and I was facing losing not only her but the rest of my family as well. Mother had always been the liaison between me and my father, and to some degree between me and my brother. The work I did with Linda helped me accomplish several things.

It helped me prepare for the imminent death of my mother. I was able to have some closure with her, to say the things that needed saying and to heal the wounds that had never been discussed. That was a blessing that allowed me to grieve her loss openly and to let her go so that she could move on and find peace.

My relationship with my mother didn't end when she died. She is often with me. I will pass through a room and get a whiff of her perfume. At first, I would search the house to find the source of the fragrance before it occurred to me that it was Mother's way of letting me know she was there. In 2002, I was looking for a house and having trouble finding one in my price range in an area where I would want to live. I finally found one and was scheduled to meet with my realtor on a Sunday morning to prepare a contract. As I was getting ready to go, a small jewelry box fell off my dresser. It wasn't sitting near the edge of the dresser, and no one was near the dresser, so my first thought was, "Someone is trying to send me a message." I picked up the box, and inside were lapel pins that belonged to my mother. I contacted Linda to find out what message Mother was trying to get to me. Mother told me that I was looking in the wrong direction for a house. I should go east and closer into Austin. She also said that my house would have a weird thing with water. Even with some prodding from Linda, we couldn't get an answer from Mother that was any clearer than "something weird with water." A few days later my realtor picked me up and said she was taking me to look at a new subdivision east of town. I said that was okay with me, which came as a surprise to my realtor because I had previously told her I didn't want to look in that area. The subdivision was so new that there were no model homes to look at yet. I chose a floor plan I liked and looked at a plan map to select a lot that was available. I put a check down to hold the lot and we continued looking. By the end of the day, I hadn't found anything I liked better, so we went back to the original subdivision. They had begun to frame out some of the houses, but the streets were still gravel. I asked my realtor if she would drive me out to the lot location so I could get a feel for it. As we turned the corner and I located my lot, I noticed that directly across from my home site was a water retention pond. The "weird thing with water" turned out to be my very own pond, over which I watch the sun set every day in my new home.

I have also been able to communicate with several other people close to me who have crossed over. It is so comforting to know that they are at peace and that they watch over me. They each have ways of letting me know they are with me. Sometimes I can feel a hand on my shoulder when I know I'm alone. Other times I hear a bell ringing or get a whiff of perfume. I have a set of wind chimes that hang in my house, and I often hear them chime, even when the air conditioning is turned off in the house. I know that it means someone is sending their love.

One of the most important results of the work I did with Linda involves my father. He and I had a very adversarial relationship and avoided face-to-face contact whenever possible. I knew that letting Mother be our go-between all those years had made us both very complacent about our relationship (and I use the term loosely) and that it was going to take a conscious effort to bridge the gap that had divided us for over forty years.

Working with Linda, I began to heal the pain of my childhood and forgave the man that I had made my father out to be. The truth was, I didn't even know my father. I had built him up to be this huge monster of a man who was incapable of loving me. This led me to the realization that I had played a very big part in creating the lack of communication and the feelings of animosity that existed between us. I had to start by forgiving me. Yes, I was responsible, but I had been protecting myself from something that I had perceived to be dangerous to my well-being, or my lifestyle, or whatever I felt was threatened by him. I had to come to terms with the fact that my father had done the best he could, and I had done the best I was capable of doing at that time. But I was beginning to see him in a different light. As my awareness grew, I learned new ways to behave with him, and when I knew better, I was able to do better. I started reaching out to him, to be there to help him grieve for the woman he had loved for fifty-three years. He resisted initially, but Mother was now in a position to wield more power over him, and she set a plan in action that has changed all of our lives!

About a year after Mother's death, she sent an angel named Paula to turn my father's world upside down. She taught him about unconditional love, forgiveness, and how to accept without judgment. She encouraged my dad to reach back when I reached out. Over time, we have grown to not only be able to carry on a conversation without getting angry, but we can actually enjoy one another's company. Our home, which was once filled only with resentment and fear, is now filled with love and laughter. What a gift! A surprising result has been that I now also have a more loving and active relationship with my brother and his family.

That angel named Paula is now married to my father, and she is not only a gift to Dad, but she has become very special to all of the family. Dad is happier than I've ever seen him, and her warmth has fused the family into a cohesive unit like never before.

In a recent update session with Linda, I learned that my guides and angels are pleased with the personal growth I have experienced, and they tell me I'm on the "Plan A" path. I'm sure that makes their job much easier. I've learned to stop struggling against life, and I'm getting better at working in unison with Spirit. They are also happy with the new relationship Dad and I have, and of course Mom is taking a lot of credit for putting Paula in our lives and helping this situation along!

The Loss of a Child

The loss of a child is beyond devastating, causing pain that the parents will carry for the rest of their lives. Parents frequently feel that it is just not right—we are not supposed to bury our children; the parent is always supposed to die first. Children are our future, and without them, what do we have? As parents, we believe that we must have failed our child in some way to have allowed this to happen. The death of a child can test our marriage, our faith, and our very existence, as the initial disbelief and numbness turn to anger and rage at the emotional confusion we experience. The marriage often suffers, as grief can numb the parents to the point that they no longer allow themselves to receive love, even from their partner. They may find themselves grieving in very different ways, but not having the strength nor the energy to try to understand their partner's way of grieving. This causes them to push their partner away, going deeper into the loneliness of their own grief.

Fortunately, a loss like this can also be an opportunity to strengthen your relationship, if you will allow yourself to reach out to your partner, sharing the support and love of the relationship. This strengthening of the foundation of your relationship will bring you both through the many difficult stages of grief.

With love, humanity can survive anything. Our partner's love can give us the strength to wake up and walk through the numbness of each day, even when we feel we cannot take another step. Or, when we feel that we can't possibly live through the pain of another day without our loved one, we need to look to our partner or family for strength when ours is waning. You also have the love and support of your spiritual support system. Your angels, spirit guides, and God are always with you; just knowing this can give you tremendous strength. You only need to call on them to feel their love and support, and you are never abandoned by them.

This was Cecilia's experience after the death of her thirteen-year-old daughter due to scleroderma. The span of time in which they fought for Kara's life was short, only one year, but the battle involved many ups and downs as the challenges were great, greater than her fragile body could endure in the end.

In January 1994, my twelve-year-old daughter, Kara, was diagnosed with the worst form of scleroderma. She died one year later.

Losing my only child was a fearful, painful experience. I have gone through a long healing process. There were many days of despair and disbelief that this loss had happened in my life.

As I look back to when my daughter died, I see it as a true test of the faith that I had professed to have all my life. I know that God truly pulled me through. I feel that God sent the right people and the right experiences in my life as they were needed. I kept a journal for many years after Kara's death. This journal has allowed me the opportunity to really express my disappointment and despair at what I felt God was asking me to live. Now, as I have gone back to look at this journal, I am grateful that I have it.

Six weeks after Kara's death, I wrote this:

"It's a little after 6 a.m. I open my eyes like every morning since Kara's death, and I feel disappointment and great pain. My heart hurts. Since I got off the sleeping pills two weeks ago, I have been experiencing the painful dreams I had tried to avoid. I guess you could say that I am at the emotional place of my real feelings. Medication will stop you from facing things head-on for a while, but once God gives you the courage to face your feelings and your life head-on, your strength is truly with God and yourself. After a loss like mine, we are all in a state of grief. I guess we have to come to this point to be able to continue to accept our lives as they truly are, and not as we want them to be."

I have dreamed of Kara as I know she would probably look at thirteen years old, developing into a beautiful young lady, in a pretty off-white blouse and flared pants. The blouse is fitted, with a fluted pattern all over. Her hair is smoothed back in a ponytail down her back. Her face is calm and peaceful, my beautiful Kara. I also had a dream in which Kara asked me why I "let her go to sleep."

I know that both of these dreams are the mother in me wanting to know or feel as if I did my very best. It has been so hard to go from being a mother to a child who has a bright future, to having nothing but memories.

I went through many months and years of questioning myself. My Kara died of an unstoppable disease. I know my loss is great, but I started to look around and wondered how the parents of children who die in freak accidents or at the hands of a terrible crime survive. I know the answer has to be that they go to God.

Every day I learn to lean on God more and more. This relationship with him has been what has made my new life bearable. Holidays and certain special days, I still have a hard time with, but the bad days are fewer. God has taught me to keep looking forward, and I believe that he will always be there.

I wrote a poem that explains how God's love has turned my life around:

The Window of My Mind
I close my eyes and ask for God's presence.
He comes ever so quietly, ever so peacefully and so lovingly.
He lets me see his special world, one that only He can guide my
    mind to see.
This window only He and I can open and close at will.
He calms my spirit and my soul.
He shows me love with no measure.
He lets me know I am one of his own.
This window of my mind is that special, special place where I can
    truly be me.
God's child!

I had come a long way since Kara's death four years ago, but I knew that there was more that I needed to do to help me heal. I know that God directed me to Linda. Friends with whom I worked told me about Linda Drake and how meaningful her readings were for each of them. Their information convinced me to make an appointment with her.

In my culture as an African American woman, we are taught that we must always be strong. We are not taught that it is natural to go through our own grieving process. I experienced self-judgment and shame at my weakness as I struggled with the overwhelming grief of my loss.

I really feel that God always sends the people we need in our lives when we need them. I believe that Linda was sent into my life as a beautiful instrument by God and my angels. I will always be appreciative of Linda for allowing this to be. I know that Linda has been one of the examples in my life that has shown me that God does care, God does live, and that when we open ourselves up to be used by him and his angels—oh, how much we grow and how fantastically we are connected to one another by his love.

On my first visit with Linda, I entered her lovely home and immediately felt the energy and warmth of the angels. I knew I had come to a place where it was safe to let my guard down and just be me. After introducing ourselves to each other, Linda invited me into her office, where I sat in the pink chair and spent the next thirty minutes crying.

Those who know me really well can tell you I am a woman who doesn't cry often, but I just knew that in Linda's presence showing my weakness was fine; I could feel her compassion. She has continued to help me through the years. The powerful combination of God and the angels (his, mine, and Linda's) have instilled in me a feeling of well-being and healing. The woman who first entered Linda's life several years ago had so much disappointment and unhappiness in her life. The woman who writes this today is filled with God's hope, peace, joy, and love. I know that nothing that occurs in our lives is a mistake, as every experience, every person, is a part of our spiritual path. Just writing what our friendship has done for my life is very hard to do.

I treasure the letters I have received from my clients as they tell about their experiences of saying goodbye to a loved one. Here is another example of a situation that many of us will have to face as our parents grow older and the responsibility falls on our shoulders for those left behind. The sudden death of a parent, whether from trauma or natural causes, brings about another kind of grieving. This is Kate Connolly's story.

The Sudden Death of a Parent

I am one of ten children. Raised Irish-Catholic in the Northeast, we had a very strong religious connection. My father started to attend Mass on Saturdays in addition to Sundays because my mother was spared death after losing a set of twins in a miscarriage. He had committed to never miss a Saturday Mass if she was spared, and he kept that promise.

My father, William Wallace Connolly, was a very bright man with burly red eyebrows that curled up a quarter inch and a receding hairline, with his red hair still intact until he was sixty or so. When he was fifty-two, he suffered his first heart attack. It was a pivotal moment in our lives. My mom gathered the ten of us around the dining room table with the Bible in her hand and wept that she had no idea how to provide for us if my father didn't pull through this horrible, shocking episode. We were spared—he pulled through. But it was a critical lesson for us all to learn how to fend for ourselves as we grew older.

Dad was a very compassionate and funny man who rose up the ranks of management as an engineer. He was so bright and quick with his wit. When he came into the room, he was the equivalent of Seinfeld . . . always laughter and wit.

After many years of worrying about his health, he had a triple bypass when he was fifty-nine. We just grew accustomed to never knowing the day or the time of his final departure. We knew that medicine was keeping him alive on borrowed time.

When he retired at sixty-five, he was called to sit on a jury that had to decide what to do about a man who had murdered a four-year-old child in a drunken frenzy—his girlfriend's son. This trial was very difficult for a man who had ten kids. He paced the floors constantly. On the night of the final verdict, June 20, I was supposed to drive to New Jersey from upstate New York to connect with my newlywed spouse who was then living in Washington D.C.

Since it was Thursday night, I had all my bags packed ready to sprint to the highway after work on Friday afternoon. I decided to call my mom one last time before going to bed to see how the trial went. I called her at 9 p.m., but Dad was still not home from the courthouse. At 9:45, I remember saying a prayer that I had never said before and haven't repeated since: "Dear Lord, keep all those who pass away in your care. Give them rest and joy for eternity." At 10:30, my mother called to say the police were in her kitchen. Dad had suffered a massive heart attack on the drive back from the courthouse. He had pulled the car over two miles from the house and attempted to get his nitroglycerine for relief, but never managed it. He slumped on the street against his car and died—at approximately 9:45 p.m.

I told her, "Mom, don't do anything! I'll be there as quick as a flash." Since I had already packed, I was out the door in five minutes flat. I raced down the New York thruway at 11 p.m., and a mist was rolling through the foothills to the mountains. In the mist, I saw an image of the Blessed Mother in the posture of the Pieta—holding my father in her arms. It was eerie but reassuring. I took it as a sign that he was okay, but my mother needed attention immediately.

The funeral was stressful since it was such an unexpected shock. So many people flew and drove to pay their final respects. It was like the Mayor had passed away. My father was so loved and cherished. Since then, our family doesn't enjoy reunions much anymore. It's like someone turned the light switch off. The spark isn't in the room for us.

Even though his death was in 1985, I still have unusual moments when I see something that reminds me of my dad, and I'm reassured that he's there—watching his grandsons getting stronger and bigger, watching the trials of life that his kids are enduring, and missing my mother.

I hope that I can leave a legacy of love and admiration when I depart this mortal coil. I know that I've had a great example.

The Grief of Multiple Losses

Here is an example of how multiple losses, whether the loss of a relationship or a parent, can cause grief and despair.

Grief has consumed my life for the last three years. It is all-consuming. I was plunged into grief after experiencing two major losses in my life at the very same time. The first loss was the end of a love relationship that I had wanted very much to work out. I had been immersed in this relationship with my heart, body, and soul. The ending hit me hard, and I was not prepared for the depths of despair into which I plunged. I could think of nothing else but my lost relationship. It was as if a part of me died when that relationship ended. The feelings of sadness and loss over this relationship still continue to this day, but they exist in a quieter place. In my moments of silent reflection, the emotional pain is still there.

My second loss was the loss of my mother. I don't think anyone ever prepares us for what it's like to lose a parent who is virtually a part of your life every day. The grief over losing Mom is still with me, and will always be. There isn't a day when I don't have thoughts of her or am reminded of her. The grief I feel for the loss of Mom is a different grief, because she is not here physically. The grief I feel over the loss of my relationship is almost worse, because he is here. There's an acceptance with Mom, and an inability to accept the loss of my relationship.

Webster's Dictionary defines grief as "emotional suffering caused by bereavement." I can well relate. I believed that I would never smile again, laugh again, enjoy life again, or just be me again. That was true for a time. But as with all things, time does eventually lessen the pain.

When a Death Comes Unexpectedly

Whether it is a violent death, a suicide, an accident, or an unexpected health issue, with an unexpected death there is always the initial shock. The survivors quickly find themselves in a state of disbelief, as they instinctively try to deny the very possibility of this death. The usual response is that they frequently stare blankly at the world while trying to understand what they are being told. They ask questions but can't hear the answers because of the deafening screams of "No!!!" coming from their heart, along with, "This can't be true. There must be a mistake." The sudden and instant loss of a loved one is an especially dreadful event because there is no opportunity for hugs, words of love, and goodbyes. The survivors feel cheated, as they feel there was so much left unsaid and left undone. There was no finality to their loved one's life. Without closure, even after the funeral, the survivors keep expecting the loved one to walk through the door and say it was all a mistake. They may feel that they are caught up in a raging river of emotions over which they have no control. It may even bring up emotions they have never felt before and don't know how to express, such as anger, fear, or sadness. Foreign as these emotions may seem to the survivors, this is a normal part of grief. They must give themselves time to move through the grieving process.

Because of the unexpected circumstances of the death, the survivors often experience overwhelming feelings of responsibility and guilt. "If only I'd been there . . . What if . . . ? Why didn't . . . ?" The questions abound, but all without answers. The death of their loved one is not the survivor's burden to carry. It is important to remember, at a time such as this, that no death is without purpose. We often hear that "it was an untimely death," but Spirit tells me that we do not die until it is our time. Whether the situation involves a soldier on the battlefield, a car accident, a heart attack, or a suicide, if it is not our time, we will not go. We often hear of car wrecks or plane crashes in which there is one miraculous survivor. It was *not* that person's time to die; the person had unfinished business. Our soul/higher self holds a ticking clock. The approximate times of our birth and death are set, but there are also windows of opportunity through which we can leave. This determination of timing to exit through one of these windows is made by our soul/higher self.

Finding peace with this type of situation can be difficult, but it is important to the grieving process. You may feel there was so much left unsaid, but please remember that your loved one can still hear you, even if you cannot see the person in physical form.

In this next story, Pat, a client of mine who has become a dear friend, will share with you her experience of the unexpected death of her daughter.

Early on a warm August morning, while paying bills, I took notice of a fatal accident reported on TV that had just happened. The reporter advised all to detour and said that it was a very suspicious accident. I watched this with sadness but did not suspect it to be anyone I knew.

It was Tuesday, August 1, 2000, and my niece Debbie was visiting us for the first time in twenty-seven years. I mentioned to her that there was a fatality on Highway 67. It didn't occur to me that this was the highway that ran in front of my daughter Kim's condo. Kim had called earlier to say she was on her way over to my house to visit with Debbie before going to work. As the time passed, I remember wondering where she was, as she had only been forty-five minutes away when she called.

Kim was the youngest of our three children. Life seemed to be improving for Kim. She had gotten a new job and had just worked her first day, and really loved it. She had a bachelor's degree in pre-med as well as a law degree and had planned on entering forensic school in September. Her new job was in neurology research.

Kim was in the process of divorcing and was also preparing to move into our home for a short time. She had stopped at her old condo after work to pick up a few more things. She was very tired and had lain down to rest after a strenuous day and fallen asleep. I felt a bit concerned about her staying there for the night. When I had visited her condo just days before, I had a strange feeling of death in that place. The man that would eventually kill her had been harassing her constantly—looking though her windows, causing her to have to keep her blinds pulled. He had waited outside her door before and beaten her badly. She was very frightened of him and would go into an instant asthma attack at his appearance. He would ring her doorbell incessantly and call her phone. He had broken into her condo and gotten information from her computer and had stolen her phone and address book. This deranged character had been harassing her for six months.

Almost a week prior, on Wednesday, July 28, 2000, when I was visiting Kim, I was trying to persuade her to move, and he was circling the condo, looking through the windows. She was afraid to even go out the door. I wanted to call the sheriff, but she insisted on doing it, as he had made it clear to her that he would kill anyone responsible for sending him back to jail. The sheriff caught him there and arrested him.

I wasn't aware of how horrible his viciousness was, but Kim admitted that he told her he had killed another woman and gotten away with it.

The sheriff arrested the man and kept him in jail as long as possible without a charge and conviction. He was released that Saturday.

At 6:25 a.m. on Tuesday, it had been so long since Kim called that we were beginning to get worried. My niece Debbie was calling trying to find out who the fatality was. She had to make about ten calls before she asked, "Was this a woman? Was it Kim Byers?"

In the meantime, at 6:35 a.m., the killer called me, angry and harassing me. "How is Kim? You thought you could keep us apart." He then began talking in evil tones, and I said, "If you want to talk to me you'd better be nicer."

At that time, Debbie was told it was Kim who had been killed. She screamed and handed me the phone. I slammed down the phone with my daughter's killer, not remembering all that he said, information that would have been useful later.

My whole world stopped. Total shock engulfed my soul and body. My world would be changed forever. I longed to hear Kim's voice—it seemed so important to me. I searched through tapes for something that held the sound of her voice, the sound I would never hear again. I would no longer be able to hold my beautiful daughter with the loving heart. I longed to hear her say again, "I love my mommy," in her cute way as she hugged me. I would never again have the moments of a mother and daughter going out to eat, shopping, or just being together. I would only have memories of this tall, willowy beauty, whom I so admired, as she gracefully skated on her in-line skates or on her surfboard on the ocean waves, or walked tall, looking like a model.

We soon discovered that Kim's truck had been forced off the road into an embankment, and she had died instantly.

Kim's funeral service was held five days later, with her brother doing the eulogy. I was hardly aware of anything, only appreciating the people who cared enough to attend. After the funeral I remained in a state of numbness. I was looking in all directions for answers, not knowing where to turn. My dearest friend, Elizabeth, had rented a house on a northern beach in California. I drove up to spend a week as I tried to escape the horror of my life. The change of scenery was little help.

In October of that same year, at a psychic fair, I met Linda Drake. She was so beautiful, with her black hair shining and a jewel-blue dress. I was drawn to her, and she immediately put me at ease as soon as she started talking to me. She immediately picked up on Kim's death, assuring me that my daughter was with me. She gave me messages from Kim that only Kim and I would understand. She explained how Kim was continuing to give me the big hugs I loved so much, just as she had done before her death. Linda's messages from Kim and her compassion gave me so much comfort, but of course they did not obliterate the pain, as that is a lifetime sentence.

After four and a half years, the pain is still excruciating! Only one who has endured a tragic loss such as this can know the constant tug of a mother's heart. Often it only takes a word, or a scene, to conjure up emotions without explanation. The pain in the pit of my stomach is a constant companion. I am always looking for answers. I know Kim would want us to go on living, just remembering her with a smile, but this is too big for me. The Christian beliefs within me are battling with the anger and hatred I feel for this man who intentionally killed my daughter, plunging me into the darkness of my grief. I quickly learned that I have to give my pain to God, as this burden of grief is too big for me to carry.

Kim's sister, Kat, has been my rock, along with other family members, and my close friend Elizabeth has become my support, to help me continue on with my life when I truly feel I cannot. How grateful I am! Kat has suffered the same pain as I, so she has a personal understanding of the emotional trauma that I experienced. Kat is very spiritually gifted, as she began seeing visual signs of Kimberly's spirit around her during that first year and still does.

As part of our healing, Kat and I have each built memory gardens for Kim, hers in Texas and mine in California. This gives us a place to take our grief. We sit with Kim and our memories, as we meditate, giving our hearts and minds time to heal.

My world has changed forever, and I know that I must go on, but sometimes I wonder how this is possible when such a large part of me is dead.

Linda's valuable counsel has helped me understand the path, the purpose, and the patterns of our lives. She gave me the invaluable understanding that we *are* all still together—just not in physical body. Her spiritual wisdom has become my lifeline, as I reach out to her in times of weakness. She has helped me find the God within me and my precious Kim beside me.

The Progression of My Healing

April 1,3/09

Aug 1/12 still at this level

First Year—Total shock! I was overcome with feelings of guilt every time I had a happy thought or laughed. I could not tolerate TV, radio, music, any noise, or crowds. I stayed very withdrawn. The solitude seemed to be a comfort for me, along with my many hours of prayer.

I did this going shopping to try and heal. But had this reactions 2010

Second Year—I finally forced myself to go into a store, Macy's, and bought a pair of shoes. I was amazed at how good it felt. I was beginning to see my spark of life returning, if ever so slight, but without warning I could uncontrollably fall into the void of my emotional grief.

Aug 1/12 where I am now

Third Year—I still didn't ask anyone over. I had no desire to celebrate holidays or other energy-consuming pleasures, but I knew I had come a long way. I could go grocery shopping and stroll through the mall, but there was still a feeling of numbness about me. I felt like I was disconnected from everyone around me, existing in a different dimension, having no desire to participate in life.

This happened during 2nd year to help others. But when their live started forming, the calls stop. I felt alone It was also helping me.

Fourth Year—I live again!! At times over the past three years, I felt that there was no purpose for my existence, but I now feel God is showing me my purpose. I now see how my lesson with grief has given me a strength I didn't realize I had. I seem to be placed in people's lives after painful things have happened to them. I feel this is my way to help others with the compassion and wisdom that I have gained through my own experience. I feel good about what I have to give.

This is me from the start. about Carly. I not still cannot find a place of forgiveness

Because of my loss I experienced a tremendous spiritual growth that I attribute to my daughter Kim. I have had to do a lot of soul-searching to find my true spirit. I had to come to a place of forgiveness to find peace within my heart. I feel that this is what God desires for me.

to find peace in my heart. I feel strongly about God wanting this for me. this point is driving me to reach each year 1,2 and 3 still why I cannot reach I am in year1,2 and 3 still yet still I am Aug 1, 2012 Debbie

chapter ten
The Grief of Suicide

Those who have experienced the loss of a loved one through suicide tell me it is the *most* disturbing loss, if one loss can be called more disturbing than another. With suicide there are so many unanswered questions and there is always the guilt that those left behind feel for not having done something more. It is often a very misunderstood choice. If the person was battling a fatal health issue, it is more easily understood than if they had simply grown weary of the battle and were ready to pass. Often the battle that rages within someone that commits suicide cannot be seen by outsiders. Addictions, severe depression, schizophrenia, bipolar disorder, and other mental/emotional problems may lead people to this final, fatal choice. Something in their lives devastates them to the point that they believe that death is the only answer. Whether it is a well-thought-out plan or spur of the moment, in the person's mind it becomes their only escape from the pain.

I am very aware of what many religions teach about the horrendous judgment set aside for those who make the choice of suicide. I disagree with many of them. There, I said it. Judge me if you will, but I have been taught by Spirit to go to God in prayer when I need answers, so I have. The first time I sat with a group of family members who had been left behind in a sad state of confusion and shock, I felt helpless, not having any answers. Prayer was the best thing I could offer.

I have since been taught that prayer is the most important thing we can do for the family, as well as for the soul that has just passed over. The soul needs our prayers to assist it through its healing transition. I have spoken with Spirit many times about the subject of suicide. I have found that Spirit has a way of putting me in the right place at the time that I am needed. I now see how we each become God's arms of comfort, reaching out to those in need. I sometimes question Spirit's faith in me, but I am frequently used as Spirit's channel of messages to help the family better understand the situation. When the realization of their loss sets in, the family is often full of questions. Some of these questions they may be afraid to ask, but they still need to find the answers.

For instance:

What happens to the soul of their loved one after committing suicide?
Will they be punished or burn in hell for taking their own life?
Will I ever see them again, and if I go to heaven will they be there?

These are just a few of the many questions I am asked. I have gone to Spirit for the answers. This is what Spirit has given me:

Just as God has given humanity life, he has given each of you the choice of what you will create within that life. He placed the light and the darkness within you. They are partners in your life lessons. Some of you chose bigger challenges in your lives than others did. The karma that some of you carry from one lifetime to another can overpower the strength of your light, surrounding you in a place of darkness. This leaves you with little balance to support your life force. It is *your* challenge to find the light that is *your* strength. Few among you can deny having been in this place at some point in your life; therefore, do not place yourself on the throne of judgment. God will not judge souls for stumbling over the burden of their karma. Instead, he helps them up, and through his encouragement and assistance they are allowed to try again.

As these distressed souls transition into the spirit world, they must go through a healing process. Because of the negative energy they battled during their most recent lifetime, these fragile souls go through an intense healing process, making a transition to a higher vibration. There is a clearing and releasing of negativity from the soul as it is embraced in the white light of God's unconditional love. These vibrational adjustments are completed in stages, as each soul works through their healing process. The healing process they will experience as they transition into the spirit world is likened to, yet is more intense than, the process that each of your souls will experience.

I recognize the knowledge as coming from the Masters, and I thank them for the clarity. Here are some of the answers that the Masters have shared with me:

> Yes, when you die, you will be reunited with *all* of your loved ones.
>
> Many people perceive hell as a place to which you are condemned after your death, by judgment and as a consequence of your choice. The truth is, hell can be experienced on the earthly plane; hell is a place of suffering, turmoil, and darkness in which a person may find themselves trapped. What we just described is often the everyday reality for many souls that are still walking the earth today. Some are not strong enough to overcome or to endure the darkness. Souls that choose to leave their earthly lives through suicide will become their *own* judge. As a lifetime ends for the physical body of a soul, the soul will review the challenges and trials as well as the choices made along the way. A soul that leaves its earthly body through suicide has created karma through its choice. During its healing process this soul will judge itself for its weaknesses and failures, and it will gain a greater understanding of how that karma must be healed through its many future lifetimes. God's love and support gives these souls the strength and courage to return and embrace the karmic experiences of life. The journey of a soul does not end with death; the soul will experience thousands of deaths or transitions along its journey.

The Death of a Child through Suicide

For a parent, grief is painfully frightening and overwhelming with the death of a child. With suicide, the grief is compounded, as there are even more emotions attached to the seemingly senseless loss. Here is another mother's story.

> Being the mom of a wonderfully loving, caring, and creative young woman, I question daily her choice of suicide. Knowing she believed strongly that we go on to the next phase of our chosen path after we leave here is what sustains me, and, I believe, that belief is what allowed her to take her own life.
>
> Suicide is not the answer and suicide is not painless, as the popular *M*A*S*H* television theme song says—just ask any person who has had a loved one take their own life. Suicide is painful and keeps on giving that pain to those who loved the person and are left behind. It leaves gaping holes where our hearts reside. It is the most painful

thing. It does not solve the problems; it is only a way to avoid dealing with them on this plane. It leaves daily, hourly questions. It ends our ability to make hurts better.

Do I believe my daughter and God intended her life to end early? Yes. I believe she was to have died in a flood three years earlier, but hundreds of prayers saved her life that long night. I believe she had come so close to death that she knew she was to have gone then. For many reasons, the following years were so sad for her that she decided to take her life.

How do I survive now without her? I pray, I meditate, and I strive to be an instrument of God's creativity, love, and light. I have had visits from her that have helped me cope. I have seen her in my dreams and know she was the reason for the ringing phone with no one there. I have closed my eyes and held her and stroked her hair. I have questioned her and had answers given almost immediately. When I am overwhelmed with tears and feel I cannot go on, I feel her presence. I see rainbows and I know that God does not offer these for no reason. I know she's gone on to continue her good work. I know.

Ann first came to me seeking help for the terrible pain her husband was in with his cancer. While working with Dean, I also began working with her and the grief associated with the many losses in her life. Having to experience the loss of a loved one once through suicide is difficult enough, but experiencing it twice is more than a person should have to endure.

A mother's loss is difficult to put in words, but here is Ann's story.

I am certainly no stranger to losses in my life; I've had more than my share. My greatest, saddest loss was on April 2, 1986, when my oldest son, just thirty-two years old, took his life. We found out the next night when he didn't report for work. It is still a mystery to me how someone so brilliant, witty, and good-looking could reach such a level of despair. William had been very depressed for some time but tried to put up a good front for me and my husband, his stepfather. My first husband, William's father, had taken his own life in 1963. I'm sure that experience had a profound effect on William, as it had on his sister, his brother, and me.

Upon hearing the news of William's death, my first reaction was that this was a very bad dream, but in my heart I knew it was true because he could no longer endure all of the bad things that kept

happening to him each and every day. On top of many other challenges, he was looking at the prospect of his wife divorcing him and
taking his one-year-old son away. My second reaction to the bad news
was feeling very strongly that William was in God's hands now, and
no one could ever hurt him again. In those first few days, it seemed to
me that the Holy Spirit, the comforter, as promised, came upon me
and blessed me with the comfort to sustain me through that awful
time. I remained in a state of numbness and shock until shortly after
the funeral service. Several years before William's death, my husband
and I had joined a church. We devoted a lot of our time to Bible study
and worship. I now feel the timing of me being drawn back into the
church was no accident.

Many relatives and friends came to the service. They were kind
and loving but understandably didn't quite know what to say. What
do you say about the loss by suicide? There is such a misunderstood
stigma to that type of death. A week after the funeral, my husband
went back to work traveling four days a week. That is when the real
grieving began. It was simply devastating—everywhere I went and
everything I saw reminded me of William. I remember trying to go
to the grocery store a number of times in somewhat of a dazed
and numb state, a feeling of unreality. At the time, I had two really
good Bible study friends who helped me cope and would kindly and
patiently let me talk endlessly about William. This was the greatest
gift of healing I could have received. Pretty soon it became clear that
William's younger brother, Ed, who was closest to him, was obsessed
with anger and blaming me for not having saved his brother. It was
difficult enough to be grieving for one son, but now to be estranged
from another was almost unbearable. Ed's own marriage (which the
family thought was made in heaven) ended two years later because of
his obsessive anger. I learned that one of the stages of grief is anger,
and if it is never dealt with, it will fester and cause an illness within
you. This was the state that Ed was in.

In 1990, we moved when my husband's job was transferred. It
was a beautiful and wondrous change for us, bringing a new beginning. In 2001, my life again came to a halt when I was faced with
the grief of losing another loved one. After a six-month, courageous
struggle with cancer, my husband, Dean, passed away. The many
phases of grief were so very familiar, but I had a new perspective on
death that made my loss a little easier. I had done some work with
Linda before and after my husband's death. She taught me how to

keep the connection between us strong, thus easing my grief. She has helped me communicate with both William and Dean in many different ways. The sadness of my many losses is still with me, but the heaviness of grief has diminished.

My son Ed was estranged from our family for nine years, but now, thanks to God, he is back in our family, having matured in his spirituality. I pray that some day William's son Philip will come looking for his father's family. We will be awaiting his arrival.

The Loss of a Friend or Someone We Love

The following story, "Guidance through the Darkness," was written by Kay, a young woman wise beyond her years. This is her experience of losing someone she loved to the darkness of suicide.

I began seeing Linda in 1998, after my mother took Linda's Reiki course and told me that I absolutely had to meet this woman. I started going to sessions, and at first I didn't know what to expect. I remember our first meeting, and how she sat in a chair across from me. As I was talking to her, she calmly asked me to wait one minute. She said she couldn't hear me very well because all of my guides were talking at the same time. Half of me thought, "Cool, I've got guides! What are they saying?" and the other half thought, "This woman's hearing voices. Maybe she's just crazy."

But my doubts were swiftly put to rest as she gave each guide their turn to speak, relating to me their concerns. They were so accurate that no one could have guessed them. It wasn't like a daily horoscope in the paper, which uses a wide net of generalizations to get you to believe. These were things that I knew about myself, things that my guides had been speaking to me about in my heart, and I had not been listening. Linda then told me that I had a lot of black around my heart. I didn't know if I should get up and leave in a huff or respond with, "Well, you are hearing voices, lady!" But she explained to me about the chakra system and Reiki, and that the darkness was a blockage and not an insult. After she worked on my chakras the first time, I was hooked. I had to know more. I wanted to be just like her, and to help others feel this way. Ever since, I have been devoted to the practice of Reiki and have become a level 2 Reiki practitioner. I hope to be a Reiki Master soon.

Little did I know then, however, how this process and this woman would help me through the hardest time of my life. I was fifteen when

I first started dating Jerry; he was a year older than I was. Everyone who knew him loved him. He lived life with such vivacity and courage that being around him was a natural high. It was also quite an adrenaline rush, especially when he was driving his Mustang Cobra at 110 mph on the freeway (a thought that now fills me with terror and bewilderment at why on earth we would do that). He struggled with depression and drug issues as well, but he was not a "bad seed." In fact, he was the opposite—he was an "indigo child." These are souls with especially high energy vibrations and special gifts who are sent to raise the vibrations and consciousness of others around them. There is no doubt that this is what he did. He was a genius when it came to math, computers, and science. His intense spirit radiated from him at all times. People were inexplicably drawn to him, like moths to a flame. I felt so blessed to love him and to have his love. Even though it was young love, it was a great love indeed. But there is a dark side to being an indigo child. Indigo children have an inherent sense of being out of place and different, which technically they are because of their higher vibration, and so they sometimes engage in lower-energy activities like drinking and drugs, and are prone to being depressed. They are also, unfortunately, prone to suicide.

I was out of town when it happened. I received a call from a friend saying, "I don't know if it's true, but I heard that Jerry tried to kill himself." I knew it was true. I had been especially worried about him that day. I hung up the phone, and it immediately rang again. It was my mother, telling me that I needed to come back to the condo. All I could ask was, "How did he do it?" She didn't want to tell me anything until I got there, but I kept asking and finally she answered, "Honey, he tried to hang himself." I banged my fist against the car window. Hanging is about punishment, about paying for a crime. The problem with suicide is all the questions, questions no one can ever really answer. I do not want to go into all of the reasons I think Jerry felt he had to punish himself, but I know that one of them was because he had cheated on me while we were in a long-distance relationship. He also felt that he had betrayed his own gifts and potential. Now he was in the hospital, and had been given a period of twenty-four hours to wake up. He would not, no matter how much we begged him to. The only response they could get from him while he lay there on life support was at the sound of my voice; his heart rate would rise. He passed away on June 7, 2000. He was eighteen years old. I was left with feelings of unbearable grief, anger, betrayal, and bewilderment. Not only had he left without saying why, but I couldn't confront him about his cheating. My heart was broken in two ways, and I could not talk to him about either.

Linda was very involved and present during those hard times. She was at my house, supporting me like a member of the family. She had met with Jerry once, and recognized him as an indigo child. Of course, after he died, all I wanted to do was talk to him. In my sessions with Linda, he would come, but at first it was extremely difficult for him to do so. He could only stay for a moment, usually to tell me, "I love you and I'm sorry." Linda explained to me about the different levels of consciousness after death and how when you leave the life you are in you don't leave your issues behind. You must work through them in order to ascend the ladder to heaven, to be reunited with God. Before, I had been working under the presumption that after death it was much more of a split escalator: heaven up, hell down. But Linda helped me see that when we leave this body, it takes some work to get back to the place where God is, where we all originally started. Some souls don't do the work, or are so caught up in their life's dark aftermath that they may not be able to get there without a lot of help from angels and spirit guides.

Slowly, though, Jerry's presence in our sessions grew stronger. Through Linda's mediation, I was able to ask the questions that people say can never be answered. I was able to work through the fact that he cheated on me, and hurt me so badly. I was able to ask him why. I was able to scream at him, and to release my anger. But most of all, I was able to understand. If I had never met Linda, my perspective would probably be that my boyfriend cheated on me, killed himself, and had probably gone to hell. I would not have gotten the closure I needed so badly, to speak to him about being unfaithful, and what that had to do with his death. I was so torn between feeling the loss of my first true love and wanting to remember him lovingly, and the feelings of hurt, betrayal, and anger at what he had done by taking his life. That combined with the overwhelming grief at his loss was nearly enough to level me. I honestly don't know if I would have survived without Linda's help.

Now when I see Linda, Jerry is always there. He has made it through all the levels and is now united with God. He will stand beside the table when Linda does Reiki on me, and, as unbelievable as it sounds, he lifts my left hand up from the table and holds it suspended in the air. He raises it through slow, tiny increments until my hand is about eight or nine inches off the table. I am able to feel him holding it. Then, when it comes time for him to leave, he slowly places my hand down, until it rests gently over my heart. He also has informed me, through Linda, that he has taken on the spiritual job of helping other souls that have committed suicide find their way through the darkness. Fortunately, I had an angel in this world to guide me through mine.

This story is another example of how suicide affects those left behind.

When I was twenty-two, one of my dearest friends committed suicide. Richard was only twenty-six at the time. Thirty-five years have passed since that overcast day when Richard hung himself. Every year on the anniversary of his death, I find myself thinking of him. I wonder what his life would have been like had he lived: Richard at thirty . . . at forty . . . at sixty . . . Richard getting married . . . Richard posing with his family . . . Richard playing with his grandkids. I've had a whole life-time to wonder about him.

It took me years to come to terms with his death. Suicide creates a tidal wave of grief, a wall of such sadness that it washes away everything in its path. It's difficult to keep from drowning, from being sucked under by the pain. The grief you feel with suicide is so overwhelming. It includes anger as well as anguish. For a long time, I felt guilty about how angry I was with Richard for killing himself.

Suicide haunts you with questions that have no clear-cut answers: Why? Why did he have to commit suicide? Why couldn't he have found another way out of his problems? And what if? What if someone had intervened in time? Could they have stopped his death from happening?

I kept imagining what the last few hours of his life had been like. I replayed them over and over again in my brain like an endless loop of tape. Richard's suicide only happened once for him, but for his survivors, it happened continuously. It took me years before I could finally unplug that tape without guilt and pain.

chapter eleven

Grieving the Loss of a Relationship

Not many of us have escaped the devastation of a failed marriage or significant relationship, but few books address the grief we frequently experience when faced with this situation. Whether the choice to end the relationship was yours or your partner's, you often experience the same stages of grief as you would in the case of the loss of a loved one through death. This is understandable because you have actually lost something that once held, or presently holds, great importance to you.

The following is one such story about grieving the loss of a relationship. I received an urgent call from Sally, one of my longtime clients, saying that I just had to see her friend as soon as possible. Sally brought Maria into my office, thanked me, and said, "She needs your help. Just do your thing." This is Maria's story.

I would never have believed I would be writing a story such as this about my life, but it became my reality.

As my husband, Ben, was rushing out the door to go to work, he stopped at the door and asked if we could meet for a late dinner at our favorite restaurant. We hadn't spent much time together lately, as he had been working such long hours, so I was thrilled at the invitation. I went about my day with a feeling of excitement. I spent two hours picking out what I would wear and preparing for our "date." When I reached the restaurant, he was already there and had chosen a table for us in the corner. How romantic, I thought. I was impressed at how thoughtful he was to have ordered us drinks. After several drinks, we ordered our dinner. Then straight out of the blue he said, "Maria, I want a divorce." I sat stunned for a moment, trying to comprehend what I had just heard. He must be joking, I thought, as I waited for his laughter. With no emotion, he just stared at me, waiting for my response. His words kept echoing through my mind. I thought, what is he talking about? We love each other.

Our dinner came, and he ate as if he had no recognition that a bomb had just exploded in my face. I just sat in shock as he casually began explaining to me that he had been unhappy for quite some time and felt it was time to move on with his life, as calm and unfeeling as that. His voice droned on, sounding as if it was coming from a long distance away, as he began to share his plan for our divorce. Coming out of my stupor, it dawned on me that this whole evening, including his devastating statement, was premeditated. It wasn't coming from a rush of emotion but was, as most of his life was, a well-thought-out plan.

This was only the beginning of what would be years of devastating pain, anguish, and grief over the loss of the person I believed to be my lifelong partner. Ben and I had been married for eight years. It was my first marriage and his second. I was ten years younger than he and just kind of followed his lead (control) as to what our life was to hold. Looking back now, I wouldn't say our marriage was perfect, but it had become a comfort zone for me. I loved Ben with all my heart. I couldn't imagine a life without him. Ben was very successful and admired in the medical community. My life had been devoted to being "Ben's wife." That had become my job, my purpose in life. I felt a security in our marriage. My parents had divorced when I was young, so I never really witnessed a successful relationship to pattern my marriage after, so I adopted the "June Cleaver attitude" from the *Leave It to Beaver* show.

For the first month following Ben's announcement, I just walked around in a daze interwoven with bouts of uncontrollable tears. Ben was quick to efficiently pack his things and move to an apartment. I felt lost as I stumbled around the house, "our home," which I had dreamed of filling with love and happiness for the rest of our lives. At times I just felt numb, which I now see as a blessing, because when the numbness would wear off, the raw emotions were too much to bear. I first began with a feeling of guilt that it was my fault, that I had not been able to make Ben happy. There must be something terribly wrong with me that Ben could not love me when I loved him so much. I constantly questioned what I had done wrong. How had I failed him? A failure, that's what I was. I carried the shame that I had failed my husband, my marriage, myself. In desperation I searched my mind . . . what could I possibly do to get him back? Anything, just so he would come back to me. I would change whatever I had to just to make him love me again. I felt I could not exist without him. He was my whole life.

As the days and weeks dragged by, it became obvious that this was all real and he was not coming back to me. I was soon served with divorce papers, which I refused to open, seeing them as one more knife to drive into my heart. My emotions were uncontrollable. I avoided going out in public for fear that I would fall apart at the drop of a hat. Each day I had to make a constant effort to hang on to what strength I had. My emotions of loss, sadness, guilt, shame, and helplessness became like a vortex in which I spiraled to the depths of despair. I still remember the day that the emotion of anger hit. It took a while, because I carried such a burden of guilt at my failures, but I woke up one day and the numbness was gone and replaced with anger. The anger consumed me: anger at Ben and his choices, anger at life and at God for allowing this to happen to me, anger at myself for not deserving love. What a roller coaster of emotions I was on. When I finally reached out to my friends, they became my lifesavers. They recognized the state of my depression and convinced me to go to my physician for antidepression medication. This was difficult, because I had to admit to myself and my physician the situation I was in. That medication saved my life; it calmed my emotions enough that I was able to step back into my life and begin functioning again.

One of my friends referred me to Linda. She didn't explain what Linda did; she just told me to go. At our first appointment, Linda patiently let me spill my guts as she compassionately reassured me that there was a light at the end of the tunnel. I just hoped she wasn't talking about the one we see when we die, because I had truly considered suicide. From that first appointment I knew she could help me. I left feeling a balance within me that I hadn't felt in a long time. Whatever energy she used worked to get me back on track. Through our weekly appointments that followed, she helped me get through the many emotions that I was encountering each day. I went through six months of emotional hell, praying that things would get better after the divorce was final. Unfortunately, just about the time that I felt I had control of my life again, I discovered that Ben had been having an affair for over two years prior to our separation. This threw me back into the depths of emotional despair, which I am not sure I would have emerged from without Linda's help. I beat myself up with all of the questions you ask yourself: How could I have been so stupid not to have seen or suspected something? In looking back, all of the obvious signs were there. I just hadn't wanted to see them. Whom do I blame, Ben or myself?

There were days when the loneliness was unbearable. The pain of my loss just stabbed at my heart. Then there were times when my anger at Ben's choices just ate at me, leaving me feeling abandoned, betrayed, and unworthy of love. Linda gave me the tools to find my strength, to heal my wounded spirit, and to make the changes in my life to move forward. Yes, I still grieve the loss of someone I loved very deeply, but with Linda and God's help, I learned a lot about myself and the purpose of that relationship.

It took a while, but I overcame the belief that my whole purpose in life was to be Ben's wife and I reached deep within me and found Maria. I am very proud of the person I have become.

When working with another one of my clients, we were discussing the grief that we experience when we go through a divorce. Few people understand the grief of this type of loss, so they are not prepared for the mix of uncontrollable emotions they experience. Here is her story.

I couldn't stop crying and I had no idea why. I am a logical person and I had wanted and fought for this divorce. After three children and fifteen years of physical and verbal abuse, the "marriage" was finally, officially over. I was very uncomfortable with all of the emotions I was feeling. Being the logical person that I am, I got up and went out to mow the grass while I cried. I knew I felt like a failure and I knew I felt terribly sad, but it didn't fit my mental model—I should have been overjoyed.

That was twenty-five years and many spiritual miles ago. At that time, instead of dealing with my emotions, I just walled them off. It never entered my logical brain that I was grieving. I didn't know about dichotomy, or the existence of two opposing forces or ideas at the same time. Over the years I have come to know that walling off emotions doesn't mean they're gone. It simply means that they are festering under the surface. There was so much to grieve—mainly the loss of the dream of the family unit. I didn't give myself any time to process the losses and went directly on with my busy life. I wish I had given myself the gift of time and space to simply allow and be with my emotions.

As we all know, the universe gives us another chance at the unlearned lesson. A few months ago my father died, and two months later my beloved husband died after a five-year battle with cancer. I was given the gift from the universe to know and work with Linda and my spiritual support group to be able to let myself finally grieve not only the recent deaths but all the other losses in my life that had formed an emotional blockage over my heart.

I am still "in the process" of grieving, but would like the reader to consider mentioning to anyone going through a separation or a divorce that grief is certainly a component for everyone, including the children. It is important that you acknowledge your loss and all of the emotional grieving that will follow. The lawyers won't mention it, because it's not their job. I'm not sure that I could have heard this advice during the divorce, but it would have planted a seed. God bless!

I thank Kathy for sharing the wisdom she has gained. We grieve the loss of our relationships, whether they are marriages or friendships. Each relationship fills a need we have in our lives. For all of us, the loss of someone we care about, or even once cared about, leaves a scar, as our hearts have been wounded and must be given the opportunity to heal. This healing often involves many of the same stages of grief. Allow yourself to move through theses stages without judgment of yourself or others.

Grieving Our Many Losses

When Donna first came for a session with me, she was desperately looking for answers. In her quest for answers and healing, Donna discovered the beautiful person within her.

There was a period in my life some years ago when I was faced with one devastating loss after another in a rather short period of time.

It began with the ending of a most special and meaningful fifteen-year friendship with the best friend I'd ever known in my entire life.

We had the most soulful connection and endearing relationship since the moment we'd met. She was like a sister to me, and we loved each other heart and soul. I thought we'd be friends forever! So when we had a falling out that we were unable to mend and resolve, I was crushed and heartbroken. I felt all the feelings associated with grief: shock and disbelief, anger and resentment, even guilt for not being able to make amends with her. In the end, all I felt was the deepest sadness. I felt lonely, rejected, and unloved. I could not understand how such a coveted friendship could end like it did. The fact that my dearest friend was gone was one of the hardest losses of my life to accept.

It was during this time that I became involved with a man whom I loved so deeply, so passionately, so completely and unconditionally. Our relationship lasted for eighteen months, and all I could think about was marrying him and creating a life with him. I adored him! I worshipped him! And I trusted him when he told me he loved me just as much, if not more so. When he left me for another woman, I truly felt like my world was coming apart. I was completely shocked and so deeply depressed that I could barely eat, sleep, or function throughout each day and night. I lived my life in endless despair, trying to understand how this man could have left me so suddenly for this other woman. I became obsessed with thoughts of her. What did she have that I didn't have? I could never believe that I wasn't worthy enough of this man's love . . . and she was. I began a cycle of total destruction. I felt self-doubt, self-loathing, and the lowest self-esteem I'd ever felt in my life. Not only had I lost my man, I lost all the love and respect I'd had for myself. I felt like I'd been pulled into the deepest and darkest black hole, one I simply could not climb out of for years. My pain and grief had become all-consuming.

In the midst of this grief, my beloved nineteen-year-old cat died, and I sank even lower into incredible sadness and depression. I was able to say goodbye to him with love and light in my heart, since he had become too weak and sick, but oh, how I missed him. From the moment we came into each other's lives eighteen years before, we shared a kindred connection that was filled with such devotion and unconditional love. Once again my heart was heavy with grief that wracked me.

I remember still feeling like I was in this black hole when my dear mother's struggle with a rare cancer came to an end and she died. This amazingly strong, vivacious, beautiful, funny, charismatic, bright, and shining woman (whom I was lucky enough to call my mom!) was no longer there for me to talk to, to laugh with, and to love. She, too, had suffered toward the end of her life, and so it was again with love and light that I said goodbye to her, though it was extremely difficult to do. I missed her terribly, and my heart ached for all the times we'd shared together as a family, which had meant everything in life to her. Once again I knew I had to face yet another profound loss in my life. There was more sadness . . . many tears . . . devastating grief I knew I had to heal.

It was mere months later when I decided to retire from my job after thirty years and move to Austin. My decision was somewhat difficult to make since I absolutely adored my work, but I knew it was time to leave and begin a new chapter in my life. But for months after my retirement, I felt disconnected from the world and felt like I had no purpose in life. I developed health issues, felt blocked in all areas of my life, and continued to have very little self-esteem and self-love. I was an emotional train wreck!

And then . . . I found Linda! Spirit led me to her to help me begin to heal, and all I can say is hallelujah! She (and Spirit) began to unravel all of my feelings of sadness, pain, despair, and loss by explaining to me that one of my greatest life lessons is to overcome my fear of loss and abandonment, which I had experienced very early in my childhood. Whenever I had received any kind of validation and recognition as a child, I had instantly felt loved and adored, cherished and protected. But when I was abandoned, neglected, emotionally abused, or hurt, I had felt unworthy and unloved. I see now that every loss throughout my life has torn my heart into pieces, and a part of my soul has died. Linda has helped me see clearly, and finally understand, that when someone leaves me, I don't have to feel like I'm no longer worthy of their love. They have moved on for reasons of their own that have nothing to do with me. She has helped me see that my best friend and I shifted in our friendship and it ended simply because we changed and it was time to move away from each other, no matter how hard it was to say goodbye. She has helped me see that I deserve a man in my life whom I can trust, respect, and truly love— not the man I grieved for, who lied to me and betrayed me and hurt me deeply. Linda has taught me about accepting loss without losing myself in my grief, and this has been an invaluable lesson for me . . . to honor myself and love myself in spite of my profound sadness.

Most importantly, Linda has shown me that my mother and my cat (both in spirit) are always with me! This has brought me such comfort and peace knowing that I can connect with them anytime I want to feel their presence around me. Amazingly, not long ago, I was running into a pet store to buy some birdseed and looked down to see a small stone in the shape of a heart. When I picked it up, I felt the strongest awareness of my cat, and I knew he was connecting with me! Just the other day on my walk I happened to look down and see a leaf that was in the perfect shape of a heart. Was it my sweet cat again? Maybe so! But I think it was my precious mom . . . sending her love to me.

I am still in the process of working with Linda and healing so much of my grief and emotional pain. There are times when I feel frustrated that I'm not healing more quickly and with greater ease, but Linda reminds me that I'm trying to heal a lifetime of sadness and grief in a short period of time. I keep remembering where I was in my life when I first met her, and where I am now! I am deeply blessed.

chapter twelve

The Plight of the Caretaker: What About Me?

When a loved one is terminally ill and preparing to die, taking over the responsibility of their care is a tremendous decision to make. Because there are so many decisions to be made at this time, ideally this responsibility can be shared among several family members. If that is not the case and the responsibility is given to you, bless your heart, because you will need it.

When you are the one who has the responsibility of taking care of a loved one who is terminally ill, prepare yourself, because it can be exhausting, both physically and emotionally. The difficulty of this situation is seldom addressed. When you become the caretaker, you are expected to be a rock of strength, no matter what you have to endure.

First, you have to accept the fact that your loved one is leaving you. This in itself takes time to work through psychologically and emotionally, time you may not have. Make sure you give yourself the time needed to ride the roller coaster of emotions you will experience. This will often occur on a daily basis.

Once you have a firm understanding of the situation, then you have to find a workable solution for your loved one's end-of-life care. You will need to ask some questions and consider the answers:

- What is your loved one's financial situation? What is yours?
- Do you try to stop your life to take care of them at home, and how long could you continue that?
- Could you bring hospice or a private nurse to your loved one's home or your home to assist?
- Will you place your loved one in an end-of-life nursing facility, where they can be made comfortable?

These are just a few of the many things you must take into account at this difficult time. As the primary caretaker of your loved one, it is important that you are comfortable with your decisions. Depending on your loved one's condition, the end-of-life care may be for a period of days, weeks, months, or even years.

As the family prepares for the passing of their loved one, they often stand vigil at the hospital, care facility, or home. With the roller coaster of emotions the family has just been through in accepting their imminent loss, this can be very exhausting. It is natural at this time to find yourself surrounded by conflicting emotions. In the beginning, you may have an abundance of support, but as the situation progresses, it is only natural, because of our busy lives, that your support may begin to dwindle. This is when all of the responsibility gets shifted to the shoulders of the primary caregiver. Even the best intentions and the strongest determination become exhausted when it comes to an extended illness.

One of my clients experienced this situation, which was multiplied when she became the primary caregiver for both her ailing parents at the same time. Here is Karen's story.

Looking back, I now realize that my whole life has been a series of lessons about responsibility and control. From the time I was a child, I was always taking care of others. I first began my healing work with Linda in 1999. It was through Linda's guidance that I grew to understand how my logical personality had the need to keep everyone else's lives in order and controlled because I was having such a hard time controlling my own life. Through my experiences I have found that it is much easier to focus on other people's lives than my own. As a child, I suffered the physical abuse of an often drunken father, and my parents divorced when I was young. Throughout my entire life I struggled to obtain my father's love and acceptance, but that was not to come, and the distance between us grew. My mother and I were always close, but because of my challenge with alcoholism I pushed many of my family away. My brother battled cancer for several years before he died in 2000. We had shared the care of our ailing mother, but when he died the responsibility of my mother fell totally on my shoulders. She had been ill with emphysema for many years, but after her son's death, her health quickly began to decline. The doctors were not giving her much hope, as there was very little they could do to help her at that stage of the emphysema. I made the decision to bring her to live with me. I remodeled the house to make it wheelchair accessible and for her comfort. Because of the doctor's diagnosis, I began to prepare myself for her inevitable death. My mother had always been an inspiration for me, with her spunk and never-ending sense of humor, so it was very difficult to even think about her dying, especially after just losing my brother. It was only through my spiritual beliefs that I had the strength to endure what was to come.

Over the first year we were in and out of the hospital many times. Each time I was just holding my breath and praying that she would make it through. She would lose more weight and strength with each episode. I kept telling myself that I could accept her death, but inside I knew I really couldn't. For two years we continued to make multiple trips to the hospital, as her body struggled to fight for its life. Each time I would sit diligently beside her hospital bed watching her every breath, trying to prepare myself for her death. She would be hanging on to life by a thread as her family would come to visit, not knowing if she would survive each battle. Even the doctors gave her little chance of survival. I was soon to find that no matter how strong I thought I was, the emotional ups and downs were quite traumatic. My life was on hold because I knew she was my responsibility and I had to do my best to fulfill that responsibility. I found myself continually on alert, as there was no room for failure in any way.

My mother had been with me for two years in her end-of-life struggle when I received a call from my father, who lived in Arizona. He called to tell me that my stepmother had died. Penny had been fighting a battle with cancer for three years before she finally succumbed to its grip. She was a wonderful woman who loved my father yet kept him in line. My father also admitted that he too had been diagnosed with cancer, but he couldn't remember what kind. My heart sank as I wondered, what next? When I arrived for the funeral, I began to understand that the problem was much bigger than I had anticipated. My father had evidently been suffering with dementia for some time, and my stepmother had been covering for him. I just shook my head and thought, "Bless her heart, but what do I do now?" Upon talking with my father's doctors, I discovered that the cancer and the dementia were both advanced. After lots of prayer and briefly considering the situation, I decided I had to bring him back to Texas as well. I set out to find an assisted living center that accommodated dementia patients, since I didn't know how long he would be there or how bad it might get. Thank God for my control issue, because it gave me the strength to work at getting everyone's life in order. My father quickly adjusted to the idea of his new home, but getting the car keys away from him was a little more difficult. Freedom dies hard. He even found himself a girlfriend. He always was quite a ladies' man. His cancer had progressed to the point that we were in and out of the hospital on a regular basis. Each day was spent taking one of my parents to the doctor or sitting at the hospital. What a whirlwind of a life! I didn't have time to take a breath.

Taking care of my father gave me one of the greatest gifts I could have received. Our time together gave us an opportunity to talk in a way we never had before. I began to understand how he had loved me in the only way he knew how. He was now able to express his appreciation for me and all that I was doing for him. This acknowledgment was healing for both of us. I was able to give him the forgiveness we both needed. That healing allowed me to love him unconditionally. I also began to understand that I deserved that same type of love from those around me.

During one of my father's hospital stays, I decided to replace the bed at his new home with a hospital bed, thinking he would be more comfortable as it was obvious how fast his health was declining. A few days after his return to the assisted living center, I received a call from my father to bring back his old bed. When I asked what was wrong with his new bed, he explained that his girlfriend kept falling off and he didn't want her to get hurt. Even in his final weeks, he continued to embrace the joys of life. It wasn't long before we had to put him in a hospice facility for his end-of-life care. I would like to believe that because of our healing and the spiritual beliefs I shared with him, his final crossing was done with great anticipation and ease.

The next five months would prove to be some of the most difficult of my life. Thank goodness my mother's health stabilized during my father's end-of-life period, but that was not to continue for long. We were soon back in the hospital, as she struggled for each breath. We each had resolved our issues about her death, and she was eager to cross over. Her poor body had fought its best fight. She had dwindled down to eighty-nine pounds, but her feisty sense of humor was still with her. As she got her strength back, I took her home. I had to admit defeat. I could no longer take care of my mother's needs, so we decided to have hospice care come to the house to help us. I have to confess that there were days when I was so full of anger that I had to get out of the house. It was just torture watching my mother die one breath at a time. I was angry at God for not taking her. I was mad at her body for hanging on and making her suffer. I was mad at myself for not being strong enough to accept God's will. In reality, we were so blessed, as her extended stay allowed her family and friends to have closure with her. She taught her grandchildren and great grandchildren so much about life and death, as she had the greatest attitude about both. She planned her funeral right down to the music and what she wanted to wear, as if it were her going-away party.

She was a very strong, determined woman with strength far beyond what most of us have, but we finally came to the point of accepting that it was time to transfer her to the all-too-familiar hospice facility. It had only been five months since I had walked down this hallway and sat by my father's bed as he took his last breath, and now I was back here waiting to lose my mother. I bravely gave her my permission, as I had many times before, to let go and cross into the beautiful light that was calling her, but this time I knew she was going. I knew I could not selfishly hold her back from the place of love she so desired to enter, but watching her die was so hard. *She takes her last breath and she's gone . . . now what?*

Although I thought I was prepared for her funeral, I was still in a numb daze. *I've lost both my parents. I am an orphan now.*

I will share with you some of the notes from my journal so that maybe you can understand the emotions of losing a parent or loved one.

Ravings of a Crazed Caretaker

March 8. The home health doctor comes. Mom has lost six pounds in twenty-eight days. Now she weighs only ninety-six pounds. Explanation: Her heart is pumping double time to make up for the loss of lung capacity and function. She's like a racehorse. She is literally burning up more calories than she can take in. We start talking about hospice and how to make her comfortable. She says she has lived a good life and is ready to go. I hear the words and I know what she is saying, but my insides feel like I have been hit in the stomach by a bowling ball. The doctor leaves, promising to call hospice by the end of the week and get her enrollment started.

My mind is racing. I feel nervous, anxious, and hollow. I make up an excuse to leave the house so I can be alone to cry. I call a few friends and blubber incoherently. I want to run away. I don't want to stay until the bitter end. My mother has lived with me for over three years, and for the past year and a half, I have been a full-time caretaker. Her health has declined little by little. I think dying must be a hard job. I know that it is emotionally difficult for me.

I return to the house, proclaiming that my red eyes are caused by seasonal allergies and I will feel better with a hot shower.

The admissions person from hospice arrives on Thursday. The home health aide comes to help with bathing on Friday, followed by the social worker on Saturday. My mind is trying to figure out how to escape feeling the pain of this final parental abandonment. Maybe I could look for a new house, buy another car, or change my hair color. I feel like I am in the middle of a very complicated juggling act as I try to think of anything other than the fact that the last member of my family of origin is going to someplace better and I am going to have to cope. "What about me . . . ?" I'm beginning to feel very selfish. When she is gone, my job will be over. I will no longer have to schedule everything around when to feed my mother. Then who will I be?

Mom seems to be so comfortable with all of the new changes. She begins to look forward to having all of the extras from hospice. She begins to talk about her desire to leave her pain and suffering. My nieces come to visit, and I listen while they discuss what kind of service she wants, her preference for music, and what to wear. They break the ice. Now I have something to focus on. I can plan a funeral. I need to feel in control of something, because the rest of my world is spinning on a different axis. I pray to be released from this bondage and wake up on March 18 with a new sense of peace. It is all about her and what I can do to be her advocate. This feels considerably better. I am still sad, but much more accepting and less afraid. It occurs to me that I am in the grieving mode and that my feelings are probably normal. I check it out with a few people whom I consider spiritually fit, and they concur. And as always, I receive more platitudes about "one day at a time." Trying to stay in the moment is very difficult for me on a good day, much less during this.

March 22. I am so tired. Even though I slept all night, I wake up with an emotional hangover. I wait for over twenty-five minutes for the light to creep under the door of Mother's room. I never know if she is still here. My stomach is in knots, and I am in a semiparalyzed state. This is so unfamiliar. I am the woman of action and I want to open her door, but I don't want to open her door. Eventually she awakens, and I play like this is just another day.

I go out this morning to plan her funeral. I stop at a store to purchase her "going away" outfit. I visit the funeral home, holding tightly to the preplanned contract dated in 1986. Then I order flowers. I would think I was out of body, except for the pounding headache. I am being so logical, and I feel dead inside.

Mom likes the outfit. It is purple, just as she requested. She declares it is exactly what she wanted, and we gently pack it away.

She wants me to write and edit her obit. She was so fond of the ones I wrote for my brother and my dad. Somehow, it seems a bit ghoulish to be writing this before she is gone.

March 24. Okay, the obit has been written and edited. No red marks at all. I call a friend in Dallas to see if she will come to sing "The Lord's Prayer" and "Amazing Grace" at her services. Mom is so comfortable with all of this planning, and she says it is great for her to have a total say in her last hurrah.

March 31. Mom slept for fourteen hours. I was quite concerned when she did not respond to the door bell, the dog barking, the telephone ringing, the yard man mowing, or my touch and voice. Hospice sends out a nurse who declares that her vital signs are just great. *How can that be!!* Here is a woman who can't breathe without oxygen, coughs eighteen out of twenty-four hours a day, is sleep-deprived from coughing, has an appetite that is dwindling rapidly, and needs morphine to get out of the pain. What does it take for the body to give up?

Every day seems like Groundhog Day. You know, that movie where Bill Murray woke up every morning for weeks and it was still the same day and the same people were doing the same things. I'm thinking a hit of the morphine for myself sounds good.

After not waking up until 10:45 a.m. this morning, she has gone to bed at 7:45 p.m. We prayed. Her wishes are to pass quickly and peacefully. My wishes are for her suffering to end, and I am fearful that the worst is yet to come. My heart is hurting and I am dreading more of the same. I know I will miss her greatly after caring for her for three and a half years.

April 4. There have been several times lately when Mom and I just chitchatted about her past. She shared with me a few things that she did during her life that she is not particularly proud of. She is doing a life review. Her favorite subject is her devotion to her family. She repeatedly recalls happy times from her childhood as well as recent experiences.

Hospice brings the hospital bed today, so I can more easily get her in bed. She refuses to use the bedside commode or call me when she needs to go, so she struggles to make it to the bathroom alone. I am so afraid she will fall.

April 16. I feel that I may soon lose my mind. It feels like we are having death drills. She thinks she is dying, then she makes a recovery within a few hours. Emotionally, I flip-flop between anxiety, fear, exhaustion, and anger, and then I feel guilty about feeling angry. It is hard to get myself psyched up for an event of this gravity, and then comes the amazement that once again it didn't happen. The guilt comes from wanting it to be over and thinking I shouldn't feel this way. What in the world will it take for her to shed this earthly body and make the transition? She prays continually to die and tells me every night when I tuck her into bed that she hopes it will be her last night.

April 21. Mom's friend of seventy-four years came to visit from Oklahoma. He arrived about 9 a.m., and they visited until he left at 4 p.m. During those seven hours, she was animated and vivacious. She even pulled herself together long enough to join us for breakfast with her hair combed. Thirty minutes after he left, she turned into a wet noodle. Sitting in her favorite chair, she reminded me of a tiny rag doll waiting for a little girl to play with her.

April 25. It's my brother's birthday. Since he died in 2000, we don't celebrate. Mom's condition is bad. I am feeling sick to my stomach and dizzy. I call my daughter to come help, and the hospice aide waits until she arrives. I am pasty white, but I have no other physical symptoms. Jane, the aide, thinks I am just stressed out. Jane may be right.

April 26. My daughter, Kelly, stayed the night. Thank God. Mom is barely able to get out of bed, and by nighttime, Kelly and I decide to put diapers on her and put the rails up on the bed. What a nightmare. She is mostly asleep, or in a coma. But she wakes up at 2 and again at 5 yelling that she has to get out of bed, and is pulling and yanking at the diaper. Kelly and I literally pick her up and sit her on the bedside commode.

April 27. I call hospice and tell them I can't continue night and day. They send out their charge nurse late in the afternoon. She continues to tell me that Mom's vital signs are good and she isn't unstable enough to go to the hospice hospital, but they call for an ambulance anyway because of "caregiver breakdown." The ambulance arrives at about 7 p.m. My niece Terry rides with Mom to the hospital and reports that Dorothy has been entertaining the EMS guys. Her spirit is truly amazing. It is 8 p.m. when we finally get her in and settled down. What a huge relief for me. I was feeling a huge load of incompetence. I stay with her overnight. It is a restless night.

April 28. Mom came to and was pretty coherent during the entire morning, but by the afternoon she was back to the semi-coma state. This is her fourth day without food and very little water. She has lost so much weight that she looks like a little skeleton. When I go home to take a shower and change, my emotions come roaring out of my body like a tornado. I begin to sob—not cry, but sob uncontrollably. I hear myself repeating, "Momma, Momma, Momma," over and over. It takes the better part of two hours to get myself calmed down enough to return to her room.

April 29. I don't feel that I want to spend much time away from the hospital, but I finally give up to run home for a shower, while my daughter, Kelly, stays. Thank God for the hospice rules . . . there are few. I load up the eighty-five-pound black lab so he can visit with Mom for a few minutes. I want him to know where she is. He has been pacing and missing her. Her hand is near the railing, and he gives her a big lick. Even in her one-foot-in-and-one-foot-out-of-this-world condition, her fingers automatically move to start scratching his ears. I am glad I made the decision to bring him down.

My niece Tracy arrives late, prepared to stay the night. Her company is so wonderful. The comfort of the family is awesome. But we don't sleep much. The clock ticking and the machines moaning are reminders that rest is but a dream.

April 30. Terry brings food to Tracy and me at about 9 a.m. Then Tracy departs and my daughter, Kelly, transports my son, daughter-in-law, and two-year-old granddaughter, Jordyn, to visit with Mom. Jordyn has been at the house with us since she was six weeks old, and Mom is quite attached to her.

They all leave at about 12:30 p.m., leaving only Terry and me to visit. The doctor comes in at about 1:15 p.m. Guess what? Her vitals are still good, and the doctor reports that it could be another day or two. Groan . . . I absolutely hate to see my mother suffer another minute, much less a few days.

While my niece and I are talking, I look over at Dorothy and see a radical change in her face. Her eyes are open and she is staring at something that appears to be far in the distance. I motion to Terry to watch her. At that moment, the aide comes in to give her a bath, but I stop her and tell her that I think my Mom is leaving. She goes out into the hall to find the nurse and the doctor who came in at about 2 p.m. They arrive, and the nurse lays her stethoscope onto Dorothy's chest and announces that her vitals are still good and a radical change will have to occur before she leaves. Immediately, Mom's breathing subsides, and I say, "How about now?" Then I look at the doctor and tell her that my mom is going—I can just tell from the look on her face, the change in her skin tone, and the rate of her breathing. I look at the clock and it is 2:02 p.m. Three minutes later, they pronounce her death.

I have prepared myself for hours, day, months, and even years for this event, but when it happens, I feel paralyzed. I can't cry. Numbness takes over. When my Dad died at Christopher House, the hospice facility, the chaplain came in to say a prayer with me, but the chaplain is not in on this Saturday afternoon and I feel cheated. I can't pray because I can't think.

Terry leaves to return to San Antonio, and I finish my business at the hospital. When I get home, I start calling my relatives and arranging the service. It's a good thing I preplanned everything, because I am sure that I would not have been able to manage everything. The funeral is planned for Friday in Austin, with burial in San Antonio.

I feel disconnected until my only first cousin, Tony, and his wife, Sally, arrive on Thursday afternoon. It is amazing how comforted I feel to have the last member of my family of origin arrive. It is like a breath of fresh air. Others show up early in the evening, and we gather to laugh and cry and tell humorous stories about Mom. I have never needed family like I do now. The strength of their support is such a blessing.

Don't ask me much about the funeral. I'm not sure I was there.

chapter thirteen

Reincarnation: Death Is Not the End

In several places throughout this book I have addressed the subject of reincarnation. Some of you may have a difficult time with the idea of reincarnation, as I once did. It was not part of my religious background. Because of my lack of knowledge about the subject, I was very uncomfortable with the concept. I went to Spirit in prayer asking for help, as I always do when I do not understand something. Spirit helped me understand how it was part of our soul's journey. This is part of their explanation about the purpose of reincarnation.

Spirit showed the soul's journey like a pyramid. Each step of the pyramid represents a karmic lesson related to our issues, giving us the opportunity to heal past karma that we created. If we succeed in healing the karma created in past experiences through the present challenge, we move up one step. If we fail to learn from the experience, we remain on that step or move to one on that same level with the opportunity to repeat the experience. We do this work through many lifetimes. In each lifetime we return to accomplish a karmic healing of our issues by experiencing, understanding, and healing the issues that we chose for that lifetime. We are given the opportunity to rectify the mistakes of our past. What a blessing God gives us as he shows us love, forgiveness, and patience. God is our example to learn from. When we work our way to the top, having attained an energy of unconditional love for all humanity, our reward will be to sit at the feet of God, projecting our love and support as he does. We are given the choice to remain there, or to return to earth as spirit guides, to assist others in healing the karma of their life challenges.

To help me better understand how reincarnation works, Spirit directed me to Brian Weiss's book *Many Lives, Many Masters*. This book was of great help to me, allowing me to put down my protective shield of judgment and consider the "what ifs." He has since written many books on the subject of reincarnation, which I highly recommend. Mr. Weiss helped me open my mind to understand the winding path of our soul's journey.

You may sometimes have dreams of or flashbacks to memories from previous lifetimes. You may even feel an attraction or strong interest to a place or time period in which you lived in a previous lifetime. You may even visit a city for the first time and experience a feeling of recognition and comfort, as if you had been there many times before.

An example of this happened one day when a gentleman came to me for a session. As we were talking, I kept getting flashes of the Civil War. I was seeing everything from conversations going on between people, to battles, to scenery and locations. I finally stopped our session and told him I felt he had fought in the Civil War and told him about the people and uniforms I was seeing. He didn't know what to think about me before I told him this, but, shaking his head in disbelief, he admitted that he had an unexplainable obsession with the Civil War and read everything he could on the subject. This information was great confirmation to thoughts and feelings he had been experiencing for many years.

I encourage you to read about reincarnation and further explore any feelings you might have about your past lives. You can do this through journaling about your interests. Places you feel drawn to, time periods you are interested in, and events and people from the past all may hold clues to your past lives. Go to those places or read about those people or events to see what memories you may experience. Discover the many mysteries your spirit holds of lifetimes thousands of years in the past. Doing past-life regression work is another option that is both healing and fun.

Bless the hearts of all of you who have lost a loved one. I pray that you will embrace the belief that they are still with you, as we have tried to demonstrate this for you through these many experiential stories.

Each one of our lifetimes on earth is really quite short when you consider the complete journey of our souls. Each lifetime is one chapter of a beautiful story. Our loved ones are part of our soul group, meaning the interaction of our lives together will extend over thousands of years. This gives us the opportunity to share our love with them for eternity. Even though there are brief periods when we are separated from them in physical form, our love does not die. It can still be expressed and received on the spiritual level, if you will allow it.

With this knowledge, as we work through our grief after the death of a loved one, it is not necessarily "closure" we are striving for, as the feeling of loss will remain with us forever, but rather obtaining an understanding of their soul's journey, as well as the comfort and love that our loved ones continue to give us. Death, we have learned, is not the end. It is the beginning of another phase of our existence, one that we will all experience when our time comes.

Our deceased loved ones do not want us to become so obsessed with their death that we are stuck in the depths of our grief. At that point, we build a wall around us, not allowing our family and friends to help us heal. It is at this time that we need their love and support the most, but we are often afraid to let anyone into our world. Often it is pain, guilt, anguish, or anger that we are feeling, but we cannot admit it. Denial does not help us heal; it only delays the healing. We must progress to a place of forgiveness, love, and acceptance of ourselves and others. Our deceased loved ones struggle with trying to assist us, but they can only do so much if we insist on resisting the help they send us. Yes, they would love to have us join them on the other side, but they understand if it is not our time to join them. From their perspective, they have an understanding of our life purpose and the karma we must heal in each lifetime, so they want us to complete what we came into this lifetime to accomplish. Our loved ones in spirit assist us, in many ways, to progress on our chosen paths. It is up to us to open our hearts and receive the support and guidance they are giving us.

With any type of grief, you know you are on your healing path when you think of your loved one and the previous tears are replaced with a smile, as you remember all of the wonderful memories you hold in your heart.

Some of us are the arms of comfort, while others are the backbone of strength to help the families left behind survive each day without their loved ones.

With the veil becoming thinner, I hope the time is near for all of us to be able to reach through the veil to hear the words and feel the embrace of our loved ones in spirit.

To Write to the Author

If you wish to contact the author or would like more information about this book, please write to the author in care of Llewellyn Worldwide and we will forward your request. Both the author and publisher appreciate hearing from you and learning of your enjoyment of this book and how it has helped you. Llewellyn Worldwide cannot guarantee that every letter written to the author can be answered, but all will be forwarded. Please write to:

Linda Drake
℅ Llewellyn Worldwide
2143 Wooddale Drive, Dept. 0-7387-0932-8
Woodbury, Minnesota 55125-2989, U.S.A.

Please enclose a self-addressed stamped envelope for reply, or $1.00 to cover costs. If outside U.S.A., enclose international postal reply coupon.

Many of Llewellyn's authors have websites with
additional information and resources.
For more information, please visit our website at
http://www.llewellyn.com

About You

This book is dedicated to helping you heal. As a life path healer, I am always excited to hear about the healing experiences of others.

I would love to hear your story, especially if something you read or experienced through this book has somehow played a part in helping you get through a difficult time in your life. Please share your joy with me through my website, www.lindadrakebooks.com. If you include your name and contact information, I will respond.

If you have experienced a healing event through communication with one of your loved ones in spirit and would like to share your story, you can also contact me through my website.

—Linda Drake